# THE POWER TO BE FREE

DISCOVERING LIFE IN THE
SPIRIT OF CHRIST

# FRANK MOORE

Beacon Hill Press of Kansas City
Kansas City, Missouri

Copyright 2005
by Frank Moore and Beacon Hill Press of Kansas City

ISBN 083-412-1921

Printed in the
United States of America

Cover Design: Brandon R. Hill

**Library of Congress Cataloging-in-Publication Data**

Moore, Frank, 1951-
  The power to be free : discovering life in the spirit of Christ / Frank Moore.
    p. cm.
  ISBN 0-8341-2192-1 (hardcover)
  1. Christian life. 2. Devotional calendars. I. Title.

  BV4501.3.M6545 2005
  248.4—dc22

                                                          2005012251

10  9  8  7  6  5  4  3  2  1

# ACKNOWLEDGMENTS

*Human nature causes us to think instinctively in terms of be-ing self-sufficient and self-made. Nearly everyone has a story to illustrate how "I did it all by myself." We like to think in terms of the rugged individualist or the self-made person. That's seldom the case, however. More often than not, we succeed because of a team effort or a friend or relative working quietly behind the scenes to assist us in our accomplishments.*

I borrowed the above paragraph from Day 37. It reminds me that many friends and family members worked with me to create this book.

I'd like to thank my pastor, J. K. Warrick, for giving me the vision and prompting me to write, and thanks to Stan Toler for writing the student workbook and the leader's guide.

I'm thankful to Ron Benefiel for his suggestion of the main discovery themes of purity, power, love, and character. Ron's in-fluence has fostered a positive dialogue in the church, as he has encouraged us to think about holiness in new ways.

Thanks to Judi Perry, a wonderful editor.

I'm also indebted to Bonnie Perry and the entire Beacon Hill Press of Kansas City staff for their incredible effort in di-recting and speeding up the production process of this project.

I also want to thank my parents and Sue's parents for giving us maps for The Quest during our childhood years. They set us on this journey many years ago; for that we are both eternally grateful.

Words are not adequate to thank my wonderful wife, Sue. I'm thankful for her countless hours of proofing and critiquing my writing. She's a tremendous encourager. This book is really as much her accomplishment as it is mine. Thanks, Sweetheart.

This book is dedicated to Brent, Nikki, and their family.
I pray it will map your quest to an ever-deepening
relationship with the Spirit of Christ.

# CONTENTS

# FOREWORD

Millions of readers have recently sought to answer the question, *What on earth am I here for?* I was inspired, as you may have been, by the spiritual adventure known as "Forty Days of Purpose." I came away wondering, though, *How on earth can I live a life of purpose?*

The book you hold in your hands will lead you on "The Quest"—a spiritual journey I think of as forty days of discovery—and it will help you answer that question.

My friend, Frank Moore, gently guides us to rediscover some very old truths that seem new again because of years of neglect. Those who read this book as prescribed—one chapter a day for forty days—will get excited about the rich possibilities of the Spirit-filled life and the pathway to that fullness.

Won't you join this quest and discover the life you've always longed for? The real question is, *Why on earth would you settle for anything less?*

**J. K. Warrick, Senior Pastor**
College Church of the Nazarene, Olathe, Kansas
"I came so they can have real and eternal life, more and better life than they ever dreamed of" (John 10:10, TM).

# INTRODUCTION

This book originated in an unusual way. It was sort of like taking a bite of meat that kept getting bigger the longer I chewed. What started out to be a simple editing job turned into, well, this book. Here's how it happened.

I led my Sunday School class through a 40-day study of our purpose in life. When we completed the study, we decided it had been a worthwhile process. Yet at the same time, we sensed we needed to study further into God's plans and purposes for our lives. My pastor approached me with the same conclusion our class had reached: our local church needed another organized study of God's purposes for us.

He suggested that since I've written several books on the subject, I do some minor editing of some of the material in those books for our church leaders to use in small study groups. I agreed to give it a shot. Before long, I realized that while some of my previously printed material fit the bill for this new study, I needed to add quite a bit of new material. My pastor told some of his pastor friends about the project, and before long other churches were asking if they could use the material we planned to give our study group leaders. One thing led to another, and what started out as an in-house idea for my local church expanded to a campaign for any local church that wants to join us in another pursuit of God's purpose for our lives.

Hence, this book serves as one piece of an entire local church campaign—The Quest. There are introductory videos for each week along with the workbooks and other components of the campaign. I've edited some of my previously published material where appropriate and written new material for the balance of the book. I've in no way exhausted the subject. In fact, I've hardly scratched the surface. It will take you a lifetime to explore all God has in mind for you. I'm hoping my thoughts will inspire you in a thousand different directions regarding God's plans for you.

Do me a favor. Don't read several chapters of this book at one sitting. I didn't write it to be read that way. Just read one chapter a day; use the rest of your day to think about what you've read and how to apply it to your life. I'm praying that God will expand your thinking through this 40-day period. As He does, you may be inspired to explore an entire map of new paths that He will show you.

Thanks for joining our church in The Quest. I trust you'll find your effort profitable as we study God's Word together. Let's get started.

# How can I live the life I've longed for?

## Memory Verse for the Week

*For it is by grace you have been saved, through faith—*
*and this not from yourselves, it is the gift*
*of God—not by works, so that no one can boast*
(Eph. 2:8-9).

# THE QUEST

*God did this so that men would seek him and perhaps reach out for him and find him, though he is not far from each one of us* (Acts 17:27).

INDIANA JONES thrilled millions with his adventures across the Middle East in search of the lost ark of the covenant. The ark of the covenant sat in the holy of holies, first in the wilderness Tabernacle and later in the Jerusalem Temple. Time and again, a deep-seated passion compelled Jones to make this quest to the far corners of the earth. He encountered great danger; he placed himself in harm's way on many occasions. Yet, through it all, he searched tirelessly for this ancient treasure. Indiana Jones personifies a man on a quest.

Millions of Christian believers have embarked on personal quests in recent years, each searching for the purpose of his or her life. They've gotten together in churches and homes across the land to read about and discover this purpose. They've talked about it, prayed about it, and reorganized their lives to fulfill it. That's a good thing; creatures of God discovering God's purposes for their lives will revolutionize not only individuals but entire communities of believers as well.

Perhaps we've been a bit more organized in this quest for purpose in recent days. The quest itself, however, is not new. People have been looking for and discovering God's purpose for their lives for as long as humanity has inhabited planet earth. What do you suppose prompted their search? What prompts your search? I assume, since you've picked up this discovery book, you're interested in this quest. So, where does the quest originate?

This quest is not reserved for Christian believers, you know. People from every walk of life, from every generation, from every culture and language group and nationality make this quest in their own unique ways. You read about this quest in the Bible verse at the beginning of this chapter. This verse comes from Paul's speech to the intellectuals on Mar's Hill in Athens. Mental gymnasts gathered daily to exercise their minds in various Olympic games for the brain.

## NOTHING BEATS AN ADRENALINE RUSH!

You'll find Paul's speech before this group in Acts 17:16-34. Take a minute and read it. Paul begins by recounting the various ways the Athenians sought God. He goes on to say—in our highlighted verse—God has placed clues about himself throughout creation like colored eggs hidden at Easter. God promises that those who seek Him and reach out for Him will find Him. Paul then adds that it's a very small step from seeking God to finding Him. That's the goal of the quest—close personal relationship with God. Few Christian believers know much about the early Western Church father Augustine. However, most have heard his most famous comment about the quest, "Our hearts are restless until they rest in Thee, O God."

Augustine's right, you know. God hardwired humans with searching spirits that resist rest until they find the way back to God. It's like the homing instinct of migrating birds. It's the answer to the question I asked a few paragraphs back: "What do you suppose prompted the search?" It's not a "what" question but rather a "who" question. We find the answer in God. He prompted the search. He created us with a longing to seek Him. Once we seek and find Him, does the quest end? No way! It's only beginning. You see, meeting God and entering into relationship with Him both satisfies and, at the same time, makes us increasingly hungry to know Him better. Augustine did not speak of a one-time conquest that frees us to embark on other adventures. He highlighted an adventure that consumes us for a lifetime.

It's true of you, isn't it? Haven't you already met God? Haven't you already spent time exploring God's purpose for your life? Yet, don't you hunger to experience more of this God who satisfies the deepest longings of your heart? That's because He made you that way.

God built us for discovery and adventure. A newborn discovers his or her hands and fingers. A toddler finds excitement and amazement with a new toy and the box it came in. A teenager goes automatically deaf every time his or her mother says, "Be careful." Grown-ups participate in all manner of extreme sports and spend large sums of money doing them. Why? Because God built us for discovery and adventure. Nothing beats an adrenaline rush!

Consequently, here we are—ready to begin a new chapter in our quest of discovery for a deeper walk with God. To know Him better, to understand Him more fully, to find the source of power that energizes us to live out God's purpose in our lives—that consumes us. The discoveries you make on this quest will change your life forever. They will connect you to a reality that reaches beyond this world and defies description.

These discoveries won't take you to a place you can mark on a map. They won't give you an experience you can adequately describe then file with last year's vacation photos. Discovery is not a possession you can put in your spiritual safety deposit box. I don't really know how to describe what you'll discover. You'll just have to experience it for yourself. Then you can describe it in your own words. But, I guarantee—God will amaze you!

I'm taking some things for granted as I lead you on this quest. You and I will need to be on the same page with these taken-for-granted things. Otherwise, *Houston, we have a problem.*

1. God purposefully created us; we didn't just crawl out of a sludgy marsh or morph from the animal cages at the zoo on our own.
2. God has a purpose for us living on planet earth.
3. God placed clues about himself throughout His creation.
4. God searched for us long before we ever got the idea to look for Him.
5. God wants to enter into daily personal relationship with us. This relationship involves communication on a two-way street.
6. The quest for God satisfies the deepest longing of our hearts, yet challenges us to get out our shovels and dig deeper at the same time.

If we're still on the same page with these basic beliefs, it's time to roll up our sleeves, empty the loose change from our pockets, cancel our appointments in front of the television set, and begin our quest of discovery. Expect to be amazed. There are many things in life I don't know or understand. But one thing I'm sure of: God will amaze you when you embark on a quest of discovery with Him!

# DAY 1

**Remember:**

God hardwired you for a discovery quest.

*[God] is not far from each one of us* (Acts 17:27).

# X—You Are Here

*These are written that you may believe that Jesus is the Christ, the Son of God, and that by believing you may have life in his name* (John 20:31).

LAST WEEK I went to a mall I had never been to before. Assignment one: get my bearings. I needed to establish my location in order to plot my path to the store I wanted to visit. Consequently, I walked through the large bank of glass doors and immediately began to look for a lighted, color-coded map of the entire property. As soon as I found the map, I looked for a red X with the words "You are here." Once oriented by the red X, I knew exactly how to proceed.

That illustrates the purpose of this chapter—to orient you to an entry point for your quest. Think of this chapter as your big red X saying "You are here." In the previous chapter, I listed six things I take for granted about this quest. I left one thing off the list because I wanted to give it special attention. The seventh thing absolutely necessary for you to proceed with this quest is—you must be a follower of Jesus Christ.

You see, in order to make the discoveries this book attempts to point you toward, you must, as the printed verse at the beginning of the chapter says, "believe that Jesus is the Christ, the Son of God." Only then can you have eternal life in His name. Only then can you proceed with your quest.

If you are already a believer, read the remainder of this chapter as a review of God's work in you and be thankful. If you are not yet a believer, read this chapter as a guide to discovering eternal life. The discoveries of this book require a close, personal relationship with Jesus Christ.

1. Becoming a Christian begins with repentance. Jesus' ministry involved repentance. Matt. 4:17 tells us, "From that time on Jesus began to preach, 'Repent, for the kingdom of heaven is near.'" A repentance that pleases God requires the following four elements:

   a. *Admit to yourself and God that you have done wrong in His sight.* "If we claim to be without sin, we deceive ourselves and the truth is not in us" (1 John 1:8).

   b. *Be sorry—not sorry for getting caught, but rather sorry that you disobeyed God and broke His heart.* Paul calls the first *worldly sorrow* and the second *godly sorrow.* "Yet now I am happy, not because you were made sorry, but because your sorrow led you to repentance. For you became sorrowful as God intended and so were not harmed in any way by us. Godly sorrow brings repentance that leads to salvation and leaves no regret, but worldly sorrow brings death" (2 Cor. 7:9-10).

   c. *Confess your sins to God.* "If we confess our sins, he is faithful and just and will forgive us our sins and purify us from all unrighteousness" (1 John 1:9).

   d. *Do an about-face like a soldier in military exercises.* Turn your back on your sinful ways and quit them. "Repent, then, and turn to God, so that your sins may be wiped out" (Acts 3:19).

2. Becoming a Christian requires simply trusting God for saving faith. Paul said, "I am not ashamed of the gospel, because it is the power of God for the salvation of everyone who believes: first for the Jew, then for the Gentile. For in the gospel a righteousness from God is revealed, a righteousness that is by faith from first to last, just as it

is written: 'The righteous will live by faith'" (Rom. 1:16-17). To embrace a saving faith:

a. Throw away your confidence in trying to please God by any means other than simply trusting Christ.

b. Commit yourself voluntarily to the Christ portrayed in the New Testament.

c. Embrace Christ as God's plan for your life and the only hope of your salvation. The Bible offers Abraham as a good example of saving faith. He simply believed God "and it was credited to him as righteousness" (Rom. 4:3).

3. Becoming a Christian requires that God declares you "Pardoned." That is called declaration justification. Paul said in Rom. 5:18, "Just as the result of one trespass was condemnation for all men, so also the result of one act of righteousness was justification that brings life for all men." God's justification involves the following concepts:

a. You are justified in God's sight when you trust in Christ as your personal Savior. He grants saving faith.

b. Justification is both an act of God and a state in which you live as you continue to trust Christ on a daily basis.

c. Justification takes something away and gives something. God destroys your record. He hits the delete button on His computer and completely wipes out your sinful record.

d. God justifies you in a moment. This is one of His gifts to His children. You do not gradually grow into justification. In the blink of an eye, God forgives you of all of your sins, removes your guilt, releases you from sin's penalty, declares you righteous, and makes you a new creature so you can begin to live right in His sight.

    *e.* God both forgives and forgets your sins. The Bible often speaks of His forgiveness (Matt. 26:28; Luke 24:47; Acts 2:38). Your sins would not really be taken away if He continued to remember the ways you had disobeyed Him and held them over your head like a blackmailer. "As far as the east is from the west, so far has he removed our transgressions from us" (Ps. 103:12).

4. Becoming a Christian gives you new birth or regeneration. Jesus declared to Nicodemus, "I tell you the truth, no one can see the kingdom of God unless he is born again" (John 3:3).

    *a.* New birth happens the moment you repent and have faith in Christ.

    *b.* New birth makes you a new creature. Paul describes believers as "a new creation; the old has gone, the new has come!" (2 Cor. 5:17).

    *c.* New birth restores your relationship with God to the way it was before you sinned against Him.

    *d.* New birth is not natural development or maturity but a miraculous gift from God.

    *e.* New birth makes you a child of God as He adopts you into His family. Paul says in Eph. 1:4 that God wants to adopt us as His children.

5. Becoming a Christian brings God's affirming voice that you are now His. We call this affirming voice the witness of the Spirit. Paul reminds, "The Spirit himself testifies with our spirit that we are God's children" (Rom. 8:16).

    *a.* God's voice assures you that your sins are forgiven and all is well with your soul. Some describe it as a sense of peace, others speak of release, and still others say they feel clean inside.

    *b.* God prompts other believers to tell you that they see a difference in your life.

    *c.* You look in the mirror and see that you are a new creature in God.

    *d.* God's voice becomes a down payment and guarantee that He is serious about taking you to heaven when you die.

That very quickly establishes the starting point for this quest. You must be a follower of Jesus Christ in order to make the discoveries described in this book. If you've already made that decision, great. You're ready to move on to the next chapter. If you're not yet a believer, bow your head, confess your sins to God, and ask Christ Jesus into your heart as your Savior. Once you join the family of God, you will be ready to move on with this quest of discovery.

---

# DAY 2

**Remember:**

You must be a follower of Jesus Christ to make the quest.

*By believing you . . . have life in his name* (John 20:31).

# GOT GROWTH?

*Like newborn babies, crave pure spiritual milk, so that by it you may grow up in your salvation* (1 Pet. 2:2).

IT WAS a sad sight to behold! Every time I looked out the living room window or pushed the lawn mower next to it, I just couldn't believe it—that poor little oak tree in our front yard. Don't picture a mighty oak. Rather, picture a little, scrawny excuse of a tree with misshaped limbs and misplaced yellow leaves. Yes, yellow leaves. It reminded me of Charlie Brown's Christmas tree. It stood about 8 feet tall.

We lived in an established neighborhood. All my neighbors had giant trees in their yards. One day as I stood under my neighbor's 40-foot tree, he told me something I couldn't believe. "You know our trees were planted on the same day, don't you?" Impossible!

I assumed my tree needed more attention, so I carefully nurtured it for two more years. I did everything I knew to do, but it remained sickly and small. One day I decided to end its suffering and mine; I fired up my chain saw and cut it down.

I've since learned that oak trees have taproots that need to drill deep into the ground. My lawn sat on a solid rock shelf that prevented a deep root system. My oak just couldn't grow on solid rock.

We call that phenomenon *failure to thrive*. The same thing can happen to children who do not receive adequate love and attention at an early age. Their physical and emotional growth becomes stunted; they sometimes even die. Whether it's trees or children, we naturally expect growth. We can say the same for Christian believers.

On Day 1 we explored the notion that new and seasoned believers hunger to experience more of God. Why? Because God hardwired us to seek Him. He built us for discovery and adventure. So, it's natural that after you discover your purpose in life you continue to search for something more. You may not be able to put your finger on it at first, but as time goes on, you begin to hear an inner urge, a longing, a hunger, and a drive. You feel compelled to grow in your relationship with God. Nobody has to tell you God has more for you; you already know it—from deep within. You're not unique; God made us all this way.

The Bible outlines some elements necessary for spiritual growth. Here is a partial list.

1. Participate in a variety of means of grace, such as prayer, Bible reading, meditation, corporate worship, the Lord's Supper, Christian fellowship, and fasting. Also add listening to Christian music and reading Christian literature. Organize your life around your faith.

2. Practice the presence of God in your life every day. Talk with Him throughout the day as you talk with your closest friend. Listen for His voice to direct you, and obey Him. Stop doing what He tells you to stop doing, and start doing what He tells you to do. Welcome new light from God.

3. Discipline your life to make it consistent with your commitment to Christ. This discipline applies to areas like eating habits, entertainment choices, time usage, choice of friends, responsibility to commitments, keeping your word, honesty in business dealings, responsibility with your money, and attitudes. You won't always find yourself on top of every situation. You may stumble along the way. When you do, talk to the Lord about it, get back

up, and keep walking with Christ. Help Him help you.

4. Learn to cope with life's daily circumstances. Some days you see the sun, other days you feel the rain. Learn not to gauge your level of spiritual maturity on how well things happen to be going at the time. You can live close to God when circumstances collapse around you, and you can drift when everything falls into place. Coping skills are as important to Christian living as spiritual experiences. Anticipate problems before they become unsolvable, and deal with them.

5. Commit to the Lord your past failures, appetites, weaknesses, temptations, the failures of others, and situations you cannot change. Leave all of these things in God's hands and talk to Him about them as often as they come to your mind. Becoming a Christian does not solve all of your problems any more than winning a sweepstakes brings you ultimate happiness. It does give you spiritual resources for dealing effectively with them, however. Get help from trusted Christian friends or counselors if you need it. God may work through them to help you.

6. Open your life to Kingdom priorities in each area of your life. This includes giving time and money to the cause of Christ. Give your life away in service to others. It won't seem like an obligation but a welcomed opportunity, as Jesus described in Matt. 25:31-46. His followers feed the hungry, take in strangers, clothe the needy, care for the sick and imprisoned without even noticing what they are doing. It's just a natural outgrowth of faith.

All spiritual growth centers on Christlikeness. Paul says believers have "the mind of Christ" (1 Cor. 2:16). The more time you spend with Him, reading His Word and Christian literature, listening to music about Him, fellowshipping with other believers, the more like Him you will become. He will adopt you into His family, and you will take on the family resemblance. You will naturally begin to prefer the things He prefers and shy away from what displeases Him. Your actions, attitudes, intentions, and motives will align with His purposes. As Paul said, "I want to know Christ and the power of his resurrection and the fellowship of sharing in his sufferings, becoming like him in his death" (Phil. 3:10).

Want to know if you are alive in Christ? Look in the mirror and ask yourself the question, "Got growth?"

# DAY 3

**Remember:**
Spiritual life brings growth.
*So that by it you may grow up in your salvation* (1 Pet. 2:2).

# TROUBLE IN RIVER CITY

*But Peter insisted emphatically, "Even if I have to die with you, I will never disown you." And all the others said the same* (Mark 14:31).

THOSE OF US who work on a Christian university campus enjoy the benefit of watching romances develop and blossom between our students. It's exciting to watch a young man and a young woman meet, get acquainted over time, and fall in love. My wife, Sue, and I spend many summer weekends attending our students' weddings. What could be more thrilling than two young lovers pledging themselves to one another for a lifetime? Plus, we enjoy lots of cake and punch!

The thrill of young romance sometimes gets bogged down in the challenges of life and results in crisis. I remember one particular situation when a former newlywed student stopped by our home to discuss his dilemma with me. As he described his circumstances, he said, "I can't really put my finger on it. I just know something is wrong between my wife and me. If we don't figure it out and solve the problem soon, it's going to threaten our marriage." We talked at length. I gave him my advice and prayed with him. Thankfully, he and his wife found the source of their problem and fixed it. They're still married and are now learning about parenthood.

The usual pattern of growth for new believers follows a similar path. New life in Christ begins with excitement and enthusiasm as God welcomes a new child into His family. Regular church attendance, Bible reading, and Christian fellowship mark the trail of the new believer. Along the way, new believers typically come to a realization that is similar to my newlywed student's dilemma: a painful awareness that there is a problem in their relationship with Christ. They can't always put a finger on it. They're not even willing to call it a problem at first. But, over a period of weeks or months, they come to terms with the emerging realization that there's trouble in River City with their faith walk. They fear that if they do not get to the source of the problem and solve it, their very relationship with Christ could be threatened.

Sound familiar? Have you ever had that emerging realization that something's not quite right with your spiritual walk? I sure have. As I've analyzed this phenomenon over the years, both in my own spiritual life and in the spiritual lives of friends, I've discerned several sources for this problem.

1. Sometimes you may sense things changing in your spiritual walk as it settles from the new and novel to a life pattern. That's natural. The fever-pitched level of excitement you felt at the time of spiritual new birth cannot be sustained for a lifetime. Every party must end and life must return to a routine. Don't get discouraged when your spiritual walk settles into a routine. You're normal.

2. Sometimes you will sense things changing in your spiritual walk as you go through the normal highs and lows of human life. Remember, everything on earth goes through cycles. The seasons. The leaves on the trees. The sun. The moon. The weather. And human experiences and emotions. Some days you will have the world by the tail on a downhill pull. Other days you'd just as soon stay in bed. The cycles in your spiritual walk do not necessarily signal a problem in your relationship with God. You may simply be experiencing a normal pattern of human existence.

3. Sometimes you will sense things changing in your spiritual walk as you grow in Christ. Teenagers always wonder what's happening to them as their bodies, emotions, and minds morph from childhood to adolescence. Such change in your spiritual life signals a good thing as you move from Christian babe to seasoned saint.

4. Sometimes, however, you may sense a change in your spiritual walk that is not the cooling of new emotion, a normal human cycle, or maturity. Sometimes there is a spiritual problem at a deeper level. Maybe you can't really put your finger on it at first. You just know that something has changed, and it's not for the better. Let's focus on this for a minute.

This is when you seriously ask yourself how you're going to live the life you long for. Let's tackle this problem with a series of questions like your doctor might ask when trying to diagnose a physical ailment.

- Do you hunger to return to your old sinful lifestyle and circle of friends? Probably not. That self-destructive way of living headed you toward more misery and death. You thank God every day for delivering you from your death trap.
- Is your love for God, His family, or spiritual things waning? Usually this is not the problem. Believers love God as much as they ever did. They love Him more, in fact, as they fall in love with God all over again from time to time.
- Are you slipping in your spiritual disciplines? This is not normally the problem either. Believers continue to read their Bibles, attend church services, and enjoy Christian fellowship. Christ remains the center of their priorities.

And yet, you suspicion something may be askew in your spiritual walk. What gives? You want to follow Christ more than anything. You want Kingdom priorities to govern everything you do. At the same time, you realize that you're going to need something more to help you persevere to the end. What is this something more for which you search? Where is this life you long for?

After more than three years of living and working with their Master, Peter and company determined to follow Him right into the jaws of death. No believer has uttered a more determined resolve or claimed a higher allegiance to Christ than Peter and his friends as they headed toward the Cross with their Master. Read again Mark 14:31, found at the beginning of this chapter. Peter and the others sound completely committed. They soon met trouble in River City, though, when the storm of Jesus' arrest and trial washed over them. Peter may have insisted emphatically, but his insistence wasn't enough. He needed something more in order to maintain his commitment to Christ. But what?

# DAY 4

## Remember:

We need more than resolve and determination to live the Christian life.

*But Peter insisted emphatically* (Mark 14:31).

# THE REST OF THE STORY

*On one occasion, while he was eating with them, he gave them this command: "Do not leave Jerusalem, but wait for the gift my Father promised, which you have heard me speak about. For John baptized with water, but in a few days you will be baptized with the Holy Spirit"* (Acts 1:4-5).

YESTERDAY you got a slight glimpse into the way Jesus' disciples felt as they tried to come to terms with the sharp disconnect between their promise and resolve to follow Jesus in Mark 14:31 and their actions later in that same chapter. Mark 14:50 says, "Then everyone deserted him and fled." Now read verses 66-72. Peter hung around the shadows and openly denied that he even knew Christ. Sounds like all-out, full-blown desertion to me. These actions represent the highest level of failure imaginable. How on earth could the pendulum of the disciples' lives swing so quickly from total commitment to total desertion?

Did the disciples' failure surprise Jesus? No, He predicted it right down to the smallest detail (vv. 27-30). Jesus talked to His disciples about the need for something more in their spiritual walks long before they even knew they needed it. You can read the full account of this discussion in John 14—17. Pay particular attention to John 14:29, "I have told you now *before it happens,* so that when it does happen you will believe"(emphasis added). Jesus answered a question the disciples hadn't yet asked. It's the same question we're seeking to answer in this book: How can I live the life I've longed for?

Following His resurrection, Jesus appeared to His followers on many occasions before returning to heaven. Beginning in John 20:10 and running through 21:25, we read about several of these appearances. Note Jesus' conversation with Peter in verses 15-23. Jesus lovingly restores their relationship and moves Peter past the failure of his denial during Jesus' trial.

Even though John leaves the story with Peter's reinstatement, we know the story did not end there. If it had, we'd be left wondering if Peter found all that he needed for living a victorious Christian life or if he lived the rest of his days swinging between success and failure as a follower of Jesus Christ. In Acts 1, Luke tells us the rest of the story.

It all happened so fast it seemed like an abrupt ending to the disciples. Before Jesus' resurrection appearances had hardly started, He stood on the Mount of Olives telling them good-bye. Their hearts were heavy with sorrow. They could hardly form the words to properly close their time together. How do you wrap up something like this?

Then He filled their ears and hearts with a message of promise and hope. "Do not leave Jerusalem, but wait for the gift my Father promised, which you have heard me speak about. For John baptized with water, but in a few days you will be baptized with the Holy Spirit" (Acts 1:4-5). He went on to promise a new source of power for their Christian lives: "But you will receive power when the Holy Spirit comes on you; and you will be my witnesses in Jerusalem, and in all Judea and Samaria, and to the ends of the earth" (v. 8). Again, He answered a question they had not yet asked, "How do I live the Christian life after Jesus returns to His Father?" Then, like a rocket ship off a launch pad, Jesus lifted from the ground and soon disappeared from sight. He returned to His Father; the disciples felt all alone.

Thankfully, they obeyed Jesus. They gathered back in the Upper Room where they had shared the Last Supper with Jesus 40 days earlier. They joined together in prayer. It was a unifying experience. They had experienced trying times over the past several weeks. Now, with Jesus absent from the group, they needed a new catalyst to draw them together. They prayed through each day and into the evening for more than a week. They didn't know how long they would be together like this or exactly what to expect. Jesus seemed to indicate that when His promise reached its fulfillment among them, they would have no doubt. So, they waited for something dramatic.

And something dramatic happened. On the 10th day of their prayer meeting, the heavens broke open and the promised Spirit filled them (Acts 2:1-4). It happened on the Day of Pentecost. Just as God gave marvelous signs when He instituted a new contract with Moses, He gave the disciples marvelous signs with their new contract.

When God gave Moses the Ten Commandments, the Hebrew nation put on clean clothes, prepared their hearts, and waited. On the third day, a dark cloud covered Mount Sinai. From the cloud came bright lightning, deafening thunder, and a loud trumpet blast. Smoke billowed from the mountain as fire descended from heaven. The mountain shook as if being ripped apart by an earthquake (Exod. 19:14-19). These sights and sounds signaled the presence and power of God.

The sights and sounds of Pentecost also signaled the presence and power of God. A sound like a great wind was heard, symbolizing power. Flames of fire descended upon each participant, symbolizing purity of heart. They all began proclaiming the gospel message in languages they had never learned. They hit the streets and told thousands of Jerusalem visitors about Jesus Christ. This symbolized the need to take the new gospel message to the ends of the earth, to every language group. Keep in mind, these were the same people who had displayed full-blown desertion and denial just a few days earlier. Now they were publicly telling everyone about Jesus Christ.

So how were their concerns about living as Christians after Jesus returned to His Father resolved? Jesus had certainly fulfilled His Mount of Olives promise: the Spirit came upon them in ways they could never doubt. He changed their lives forever. Acts 2 tells the rest of the story. The spiritual truths revealed in this chapter show the amazing quest of the Early Church as it took the world by storm for Christ. These truths also offer us a road map for our quest with Christ.

Everything Jesus told us during His ministry about the Spirit and everything we see happening in the Early Church following Acts 2 shows us the secret of spiritual growth, how to overcome spiritual hindrances, and how to live a victorious Christian life. You will learn more about this exciting message as you continue your quest through these days of discovery.

Our memory verse for the week reminds us that every discovery we make on this quest comes our way by God's grace. "For it is by grace you have been saved, through faith—and this not from yourselves, it is the gift of God—not by works, so that no one can boast" (Eph. 2:8-9).

You must place your faith in Him, but that faith earns you nothing. Remember, all your discoveries are gifts from God!

---

# DAY 5

## Remember:
The answer to our question is found in the Spirit of Christ.

*In a few days you will be baptized with the Holy Spirit (Acts 1:4-5).*

# DISCOVERY 1
## YOU HAVE A GUIDE.

## Memory Verse for the Week

*I will not leave you as orphans;*
*I will come to you* (John 14:18).

# A SPIRIT GUIDE

*But if I go, I will send him to you* (John 16:7).

POLICE OFFICER John Sullivan was haunted by the death of his father, Frank, for more than 30 years. Frank, a firefighter, died while trying to extinguish a large warehouse blaze. Through a strange turn of events, John made contact on his shortwave radio with the world beyond and opened a communication line with his dad. Frank gave John directions to do certain things that would change the entire chain of events, thus altering history. It's a fascinating story line. I won't say any more, because I don't want to ruin the ending if you haven't seen the popular movie *Frequency* staring Dennis Quaid and Jim Caviezel.

Science fiction? Of course. Popular? Very. We're living in a new day when it comes to talking about spirit guides. I'm old enough to remember when it was neither socially acceptable nor intellectually respectable to talk about receiving direction from "the other side." Forget that.

Today, movie stars testify on television and in popular magazine articles about their own personal spirit guides. Bookstores devote entire shelves to books telling us how to receive direction for life from the spirit world. One television personality in the current schedule of afternoon offerings claims he can contact the spirit world on behalf of his audience. He makes several "contacts" during each program and relays messages back to family members and loved ones. The audience listens with eager anticipation and cheers as these specially chosen individuals receive words of encouragement from the other side. Yes, spirit guides get top billing in popular culture these days.

These examples highlight a return in our postmodern society to acknowledging the spiritual dimension of life and to our potential as citizens of this world to receive guidance from another world. Those options have been explored extensively in science fiction movies and fantasy books. They are now receiving fresh treatments from a variety of mainstream sources.

Why has postmodern society turned its attention to the spiritual dimensions of life? The reasons are probably quite complex. But let me suggest one possibility. Science and technology received the honor and even the worship of gods in the modern age. Humanity has a problem? No problem. Science and technology will develop a solution for it.

Science and technology promised to whisk us into the carefree future world of George Jetson. I remember visiting Disneyland in 1959. One of the exhibits displayed a scientific rendition of the home of the future. I couldn't wait to grow up and live in a carefree home just like it.

But something went terribly wrong with that scientific vision. Things didn't quite materialize as anticipated. As the years unfold, we've ceased to deify science and technology. For every problem they solve, they create another one. For example, we take a pill to solve a physical problem, but the pill produces side effects. Sometimes the side effects overshadow the original problem. Or, we buy a computer program to make certain areas of our lives easier. But the new program conflicts with other programs already on our computer. The two programs enter into battle and shut down the entire computer!

As people lose faith in science and technology, they consider other answers to their spiritual needs. Hence, we find society returning to the spiritual dimension of life. Part of that emphasis involves the discussion of spirit guides.

Several years ago I taught a student named Daniel in a couple of my university classes. Daniel came from an American Indian heritage. He had been educated in his cultural traditions long before his exposure to Christianity. After becoming a Christian, Daniel saw connections between what his elders had taught him about spirit guides and the Christian understanding of the leadership of Christ's Spirit. His classmates did not see those connections the way Daniel saw them. But the students I teach today have been so influenced by their postmodern culture that they now make instant connections between the two concepts. It's not a stretch for them.

No, Christian believers do not go on television programs and attempt to communicate with deceased loved ones. Neither do they fall prey to the misguided popular notions of spirit guides. However, Christians do resonate with the idea that we can be indwelt and guided by the Spirit of Christ. When Jesus left His disciples on the Mount of Olives for His homeward journey, He promised to return to them in a spiritual way. They claimed that promise and lived the rest of their lives on earth with His indwelling presence and direction.

You, too, may claim this promise of Christ. You'll be excited to learn in our quest this week that Christ wants to indwell and direct you. His Word is true; His promises are available.

## DAY 6

**Remember:**

Christ promised us a Spirit guide.

*But if I go, I will send him to you* (John 16:7).

# WHAT'S IN A NAME?

*I will not leave you as orphans; I will come to you*
(John 14:18).

LOIS, a coed, sat in my office at the university one day last year and explained her rather complex academic problem to me. She sought my assistance, so I did my best to discover as much as I could about her. I needed as full a picture as possible so I could explore all of my options in seeking a solution. Each piece of her life story became part of the puzzle I created mentally. As our meeting ended, I took her phone number and told her I would be back in touch when I thought I had a solution to offer her.

Lois left my office, and I started making calls to employees on campus to gather more details. The details became additional puzzle pieces for her case. When I learned her maiden name, all the pieces instantly fell into place. That gave me a clear picture of her entire situation. You see, my wife, Sue, and I went to school with her mother. Her grandparents were members of our Sunday School class for many years. I knew Lois's family well, which enabled me to quickly find a solution for her problem.

A name communicates volumes. Sometimes you think you're dealing with a total stranger on the phone. You hear her name, then suddenly realize you live down the street from her or go to church with her. In my illustration, a complete family history emerged just by hearing a name.

Day 5 ended with Jesus' fulfillment of a promise He made to His disciples on the Mount of Olives before returning to His Father. When we hear Jesus tell us about the Spirit who filled the disciples at Pentecost, we assume Jesus is talking about someone completely different from himself. But is He?

The insights of this chapter could revolutionize your understanding of God and the way you relate to Him. Don't become frustrated if you have trouble grasping what I am about to say. Leaders of the Early Church struggled for several hundred years trying to make the puzzle pieces form a coherent picture from what Jesus said about the Spirit in John 14—17 and the miraculous events described in the Book of Acts. They finally got the pieces together. What they discovered may amaze you.

A NAME COMMUNICATES VOLUMES.

Previously I discussed the Spirit being the key to the disciples' concerns about living a Christian life after Jesus returned to His Father. We read about Him throughout Jesus' ministry and the rest of the New Testament. Who is the Spirit?

Think again of the verse printed at the beginning of this chapter. "I will not leave you as orphans; I will come to you" (John 14:18). As Jesus prepared His disciples for the anxiety of His departure from this world, He comforted them with the words, "I will come to you." This promise appears in the center of His discussion of the Spirit. Hold that thought.

Rom. 8:9-10 tells us, "You, however, are controlled not by the sinful nature but by the Spirit, if the Spirit of God lives in you. And if anyone does not have the Spirit of Christ, he does not belong to Christ. But if Christ is in you, . . . your body is alive because of righteousness." Paul references the Spirit and then calls Him the Spirit of God and the Spirit of Christ. Then, Paul said those who have the Spirit living in their lives have

Christ living within them. Not a friend of Christ, not a replacement for Christ, but Christ. Now hold that thought.

In Acts 16:6-7, "Paul and his companions traveled throughout the region of Phrygia and Galatia, having been kept by the Holy Spirit from preaching the word in the province of Asia. When they came to the border of Mysia, they tried to enter Bithynia, but the Spirit of Jesus would not allow them to." Paul received instruction from Jesus about the direction to take his travels. Verse 6 refers to the Spirit directing Paul; verse 7 names Him the Spirit of Jesus. Add that thought to the mix.

In Phil. 1:19, Paul named some of the difficulties he faced as a disciple of Jesus Christ. He thanked believers in Philippi for praying for him. He rejoiced in his hardships because of their prayers and because of the help of the Spirit of Jesus Christ.

Do you see what the Bible tells us in these four passages? When we hear about the Spirit's work at Pentecost in Acts 2, we're not meeting someone new. We're reconnecting in a new way with our Savior Jesus Christ. Jesus promised His disciples in their last intimate discussion before His passion that He would come to them. At their deaths? At His second coming? No, actually with the coming of the Spirit whom Paul named the Spirit of Christ!

What's in a name? Everything you know about Christ, everything you feel deep in your heart for Christ can be transferred to your understanding of the Spirit. Christ's fulfillment of His promise to send the Spirit did not connect us to another god; it brought us a new manifestation of Christ himself. The Spirit of Christ.

What does this exciting discovery mean for your spiritual quest? It means Jesus did not go back to the Father and pass you off to one of His angels for spiritual direction, strength, purity, power, and everything else you need to live the Christian life. Jesus came to earth as a human, showed you the way to the Father, died for your salvation, was raised from the dead, went back to heaven, then returned in another form. He's not just with you as a friend who walks physically by your side as He walked with His disciples; He's in your heart in a profoundly new way. The disciples first experienced the Spirit of Jesus as they interacted with the man in Israel. They later experienced His Spirit in their hearts.

What a powerful realization! What could be better than having Jesus Christ as a permanent heart guest? In a greater way than the disciples imagined, Jesus kept the promise He made to them recorded in John 14:18, "I will come to you."

Matthew begins his account of Jesus by quoting from Isa. 7:14. Jesus' name Immanuel means "God with us." Matthew ends his account by saying this same Jesus will be with us to the end of the age (28:20). Matthew could not possibly have understood what Jesus meant by that last promise until Pentecost. Then he realized that Jesus is "with" us by being "in" us through His Spirit.

## DAY 7

**Remember:**

The Spirit is really the Spirit of Christ.

*I will come to you* (John 14:18).

# WHO IS OUR GUIDE?

*And I will ask the Father, and he will give you another Counselor to be with you forever—the Spirit of truth* (John 14:16-17).

THE BIBLE begins with "In the beginning God . . ." and nowhere attempts to prove His existence. Scholars have debated the reality of His existence for millennia while the Bible takes it for granted. The Old Testament salvation narrative presents the notion of one God referred to by many different names. The New Testament narrative presents a problem by introducing us to Jesus Christ. Who is Jesus in relation to the Old Testament God? The picture becomes even more complicated when Jesus begins to talk about the Spirit. Who is the Spirit in relation to Jesus and the Old Testament God?

Put yourself in the sandals of an Early Church believer for a minute and feel the dilemma. Deut. 6:4 clearly teaches, "Hear, O Israel: The LORD our God, the LORD is one." The New Testament presents us with discussions of Father, Son, and Spirit. What's going on here? One God or three?

All three persons of the Trinity are God. They represent one God, not three. The Great Commission challenges us to "go and make disciples of all nations, baptizing them in the name of the Father and of the Son and of the Holy Spirit" (Matt. 28:19). This commission might imply baptizing new believers in three deities. However, the three names speak of a single God.

We must be careful to avoid error in our analysis. Some

people incorrectly say the one God goes by the different names of Father, Son, and Holy Spirit, as He works in our world. God the Father was the God of the Old Testament. God came to earth at the first Christmas as Christ the Son. After Christ's ascension back to heaven, God returned to earth as the Spirit. This view resembles a one-actor play where a single individual changes clothes to play the part of several characters.

This theory has serious biblical problems in that Father, Son, and Spirit are all present at the baptism of Jesus (Matt. 3:16-17), in the miracle-working power of Jesus (12:25-30), and in the closing message of Jesus to His disciples (John 14:1-30). The apostle Paul refers to the work of all three in his 2 Corinthians conclusion: "The grace of the Lord Jesus Christ, and the love of God, and the fellowship of the Holy Spirit be with you all" (13:14).

When I referred to the Spirit in the previous chapter, I was not implying that Jesus Christ, the man who walked this earth, ceased to exist when the Spirit came at Pentecost. The Spirit does, however, communicate to us the real presence of the living Christ. Hence, the Bible calls Him the Spirit of Christ.

The Bible presents us with one God represented in three Persons—Father, Son, and Spirit. We must begin with the unity of God. He is one being. It is sometimes helpful in grasping this truth to think of three persons with one essence, nature, or being. With too much emphasis on the word "three," we tend to think of three distinct gods. With too much emphasis on the word "one," we tend to think of Father becoming Son becoming Spirit. Both extremes equal error.

The Spirit of Christ, then, is a divine Person with whom we relate. He is not an impersonal spiritual force at work in a spirit kingdom as some see Him. Never equate the Spirit of Christ with "The Force" of Hollywood movies. Neither should we think of Him as a scary ghost or even a friendly one like Casper. Unfortunately, translations of the Bible that refer to

Him as a ghost cause some people to shy away from Him the way children run from monsters under their beds at night. He neither haunts nor attempts to frighten people.

As a person, we use masculine pronouns to represent Him. Never reference Him with the impersonal "it" as so many tend to do. He has intelligence, will, and emotions. He can be affected through such things as grieving, quenching, resisting, and blasphemy. He ministers to us as a person: teaching, regenerating, searching, speaking, interceding, commanding, testifying, guiding, illuminating, and revealing. We must always be careful to remember that He is fully divine with the Father and the Son. What's more, He is One with the Father and Son.

He works among us as a person. His work links closely with the work of the Father and Son, as we will see later. His presence in our lives reminds us that God is near us and in us at all times.

# DAY 8

## Remember:

The Spirit is God.

*And I will ask the Father, and he will give you another Counselor to be with you forever—the Spirit of truth* (John 14:16-17).

# A GUIDE FROM DAYS GONE BY

*Now the earth was formless and empty, darkness was over the surface of the deep, and the Spirit of God was hovering over the waters* (Gen. 1:2).

IF YOU'VE BEEN to a baseball game, you know about relief pitchers and bull pens. Often during the game a starting pitcher's arm gives out. His pitch becomes wild and unpredictable. Time for the relief pitcher. He's been warming up in the bull pen and is ready to go into the game as soon as the manager gives the signal and gets the starting pitcher off the field.

Without realizing it, many believers think of the Spirit as a relief pitcher. They think that during the earthly ministry of Jesus Christ, the Spirit warmed up and readied himself. As soon as Jesus returned to heaven, the Spirit ran onto the field to assume His presence and ministry in the Church and the world. In other words, He served as a reliever to Jesus' ministry and became a starter at Pentecost.

Nothing could be further from the truth! The Spirit is the third Person of the Trinity. Anytime you read in the Bible about God working in His world, you can rest assured that Father, Son, and Spirit are all somehow involved. The Bible may name one or the other as the subject of the event, but all three involved themselves together in every divine effort.

True, we tend to imagine the Father at work in the Old Testament, the Son at work during the Incarnation, and the Spirit at work in the church age. Nevertheless, we must never assume that only one member of the Trinity acts at any given time. God cannot be divided in this way. The Bible tells our salvation story in the three time periods of (1) Old Testament, (2) Incarnation, and (3) church age. We will look at the work of the Spirit of Christ during these three eras.

The Spirit has been actively involved in our world since its beginning. His presence permeated the entire Old Testament. He often worked in the shadows and background of ancient biblical events, but He worked nonetheless. These few examples illustrate His activity through the Old Testament era.

1. He worked with other members of the Trinity in creating the world and everything in it. Gen. 1:2 tells us that "the Spirit of God was hovering over the waters." This reminds us that all of the triune God's creation activity in Gen. 1—2 involved the Father, Son, and Spirit. The Spirit represented God's personal presence and involvement in His purposeful creation acts.

2. He inspired the writers of Scripture to record the message of God for us. Peter tells us in 2 Pet. 1:21, "For prophecy never had its origin in the will of man, but men spoke from God as they were carried along by the Holy Spirit." Think about the incredible messages from God to His people channeled through some of the great prophets like Isaiah, Jeremiah, Ezekiel, and others. The people often complained that the prophets made these messages up to disturb them. Not so. The Spirit gave them their messages. Actually, the prophets often did not themselves understand all the things they spoke for God. You can read Peter's comment on this in 1 Pet. 1:10-12.

3. He gave people special skills and abilities to accomplish His will. One of the best examples of this appears in Exod. 31:3-5 where we read that the Spirit of God filled Bezalel. Who was Bezalel? Bezalel received skill, ability, and knowledge of a variety of craftsmanships from the

Spirit for the building of the Tabernacle, the worship center for the Hebrew people during their trip from Egypt to the Promised Land. The Bible mentions only Bezalel by name. However, the Spirit inspired countless other people with skills, abilities, and various types of knowledge for doing His work on earth, especially as it related to the salvation plan for humanity.

4. He guided the leaders of Israel in the Old Testament. The Bible gives numerous examples of the Spirit coming to Israel's leaders with special knowledge, skill, or ability. The 70 elders, Balaam, Othniel, Gideon, Samson, Saul, and David all experienced the Spirit's special presence upon them, empowering them for special divine assignments. Num. 11:25 says, "Then the LORD came down in the cloud and spoke with him, and he took of the Spirit that was on him and put the Spirit on the seventy elders"; 24:2 says, "When Balaam looked out and saw Israel encamped tribe by tribe, the Spirit of God came upon him and he uttered his oracle." Other accounts are recorded in Judg. 3:10, 6:34, and 14:6, and 1 Sam. 10:10 and 16:13.

5. He spoke through the prophets about a new arrangement that would allow Him to live within human hearts. Isaiah glanced into the future to the day when God's Spirit would fill followers in spiritually fulfilling ways. "For I will pour water on the thirsty land, and streams on the dry ground; I will pour out my Spirit on your offspring, and my blessing on your descendants" (44:3). No more spiritual dryness when the Spirit comes! The prophet saw that He would come like long-awaited rain on parched soil. Those nomads of the desert knew the value of a good rain shower to the desert floor. They also anticipated the day when God would turn His dream into reality and rain showers of spiritual blessing on their parched souls.

This brief sketch of the Spirit's work in the Old Testament era only hints at the numerous ways in which He participated with us in our world. Let me challenge you to read through the Old Testament again with an eye for the Spirit's involvement in its events and messages. You'll be amazed as you see Him working quietly in the shadows.

# DAY 9

**Remember:**
The Spirit has been guiding our world and people since the beginning of time.

*And the Spirit of God was hovering over the waters* (Gen. 1:2).

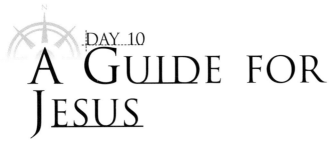

# A GUIDE FOR JESUS

*The Spirit of the Lord is on me* (Luke 4:18).

OUR MOVE to Kansas to teach at the university involved buying our first house. We bought a fixer-upper. The entire 13 years we lived in that house involved one family remodeling project after another. I'm a household handyman who loves a new challenge. Sue asked me at some point in every project, "Do you know what you're doing?" I usually didn't, but that didn't stop me! Our son Brent worked at my side most of the time. I'd like to think my goal in having him help me was something noble like passing fine craftsmanship to the next generation. To be quite honest about it, I usually needed an extra set of hands to hold a board or a chalk line. But, the projects gave us good times together and some great memories.

Brent's now married and owns his own home. He and Nikki bought a fixer-upper last year. Guess what? He did pay attention during those countless hours of working by my side. Sue and I have been quite impressed with his and Nikki's home improvements. Now if I could just get my borrowed tools back!

That reminds me of a direct relationship to the Spirit's work in the earthly life and ministry of Jesus. I read the Bible for many years before it finally dawned on me that the Spirit did not work in and with Christ for Christ's ministry alone. He demonstrated through Christ what He wants to accomplish in your life as a follower of Christ. So, as you look at the Spirit's work in the earthly life and ministry of Jesus, see how these truths apply to the way He wants to work in your life as well. It might be that just as Brent picked up handyman skills from watching me work, you can pick up spiritual insights into the way the Spirit works by watching how He worked with Jesus.

The Spirit actively participated in the earthly life and ministry of Jesus Christ. Let these examples illustrate.

1. The Spirit placed the fetus of Jesus in Mary's body (Luke 1:35). We obviously do not know how the Spirit accomplished this. We do know that Mary did not participate in any sexual activity with a divine being as Greek and Roman mythological deities often did. The Spirit found a young woman willing to allow Him to accomplish this one-time miracle through her.

2. The Spirit spoke through John the Baptist in preparing the way for Jesus. The Bible says of John, "He will be filled with the Holy Spirit even from birth" (Luke 1:15). People sometimes assume this verse refers to a pre-Pentecost example of the same thing the Spirit did for Jesus' followers on the Day of Pentecost. Not so. The ministry of John the Baptist began prior to the ministry of Jesus. Therefore, he technically preached under the old covenant just as the Old Testament prophet preached. The filling referenced here is the same type of filling we studied in our previous study where the Spirit gave Bezalel skill, ability, and knowledge for the construction of the Tabernacle. The Spirit filled John for a particular task.

3. The Spirit blessed Jesus through Simeon and Anna. Luke 2:25-40 records the two accounts of these special blessings. In this passage we see the Spirit promising the minister that he would see the long-awaited Messiah before he died. The Spirit moved over him in a special way and told him what to say to Joseph and Mary about their newborn Son.

4. The Spirit descended as a dove upon Jesus at His baptism. We've already noted that we cannot explain our triune God by saying the Father became the Son who became the Spirit. He's not different persons at different times in salvation history. This is proven in Luke 3:21-22: "When all the people were being baptized, Jesus was baptized too. And as he was praying, heaven was opened and the Holy Spirit descended on him in bodily form like a dove. And a voice came from heaven: 'You are my Son, whom I love; with you I am well pleased.'" Here we have the divine/human Jesus, the voice of the Father, and the Spirit in the form of a dove all present at Jesus' baptism.

5. The Spirit prepared Jesus for His temptation ordeal. We learn in Luke 4:1 that even though the Spirit filled Jesus, He was not exempted from temptation. Rather, the Spirit fortified and resourced Him to face the enemy of His soul. Jesus faced temptation head-on as the Spirit enabled Him.

6. Luke 4:14 tells us, "Jesus returned to Galilee in the power of the Spirit, and news about him spread through the whole countryside," showing us that the Spirit empowered Jesus for His daily ministry. His ministry involved preaching many sermons to crowds of all sizes, teaching both large groups and intimate gatherings of close followers, and working miracles of every sort. People often questioned the source of Jesus' special insights and abilities. The Spirit animated everything Jesus did.

7. The Spirit instructed Him in His teaching ministry. As a child of the Jewish tradition, Jesus would have studied the Scriptures from a very young age. He would have read the actual text and the many interpretations of the current scholars of the day. Yet, when He began His

teaching ministry, His thoughts, insights, and applications extended beyond the common knowledge of the day. He amazed crowds continually with spiritual concepts they had never read, heard, or considered before. Where did He acquire these superior concepts? Luke 4:18-21 indicates the Spirit taught Him.

8. The Spirit performed miracles with Jesus. When the Pharisees questioned Jesus about His miracle-working power, they accused Him of consorting with the devil for His powers (Matt. 12:24). Jesus answered them by saying quite the contrary. He performed His miracles with otherworldly assistance all right, but that assistance came from the Spirit: "But if I drive out demons by the Spirit of God, then the kingdom of God has come upon you" (v. 28).

9. The Spirit raised Jesus from the dead (Rom. 1:3-4). I've been guilty of imagining Jesus bursting forth from the grave at His own declaration and power like some cartoon superhero. The Bible seems to indicate, though, that the power of the Spirit raised Jesus from the dead.

10. The Spirit validated Jesus' life and ministry by filling believers to continue His work on earth.

Look back over this list. How many of these examples of the Spirit's work in Jesus' life prompt your thinking about ways He wants to work in your life as well? The Spirit did not bring you to earth through special conception or send a forerunner to prepare the world for your ministry. I doubt if a dove landed on your shoulder at baptism. However, He stands ready:

- to help you in time of temptation
- to empower you for your daily ministry
- to instruct you as you teach others about Christ
- to work in your life in unexplainable ways

In the end, just like Jesus, He will raise you from the dead to live with Him in heaven forever.

# DAY 10

**Remember:**

The Spirit actively participated in the life and ministry of Jesus Christ.

*The Spirit of the Lord is on me* (Luke 4:18).

# DAY 11
# A GUIDE FOR THE WORLD

*When he comes, he will convict the world of guilt in regard to sin and righteousness and judgment* (John 16:8).

THE HOLY SPIRIT brings God's presence to our world today. We will focus our attention in the next two chapters on the Spirit's current involvement. He so involves himself with us that we can easily divide our analysis into two categories: His work with prebelievers and His work with believers. Even though I call the first group prebelievers, it's not because I think everyone will eventually or automatically believe in Christ. I call them prebelievers because the Spirit makes them an offer of eternal salvation they can't refuse—or at least they can't if they honestly consider the alternative! The believers category will include what the Spirit does both in individual believers and in the Christian community. Let's look now at what the Spirit does with prebelievers.

Gen. 1 begins with a snapshot of the Spirit brooding over the early formation of creation the way a mother hen broods over her nest of freshly laid eggs. We often think that after the Spirit completed His creation task He ceased to brood over His world. Perhaps not. Perhaps the Spirit continues to hover over His handiwork as He sustains it day by day. Of course, we won't know the final answer to this speculation until we join Him on the other side. It seems to me that the providential unseen hand of God often works quietly in the shadows of our world to sustain it. This providential ministry could very well be a function the Spirit fulfills as He brings God's presence near His creation.

Every living thing except God requires a source of energy to sustain it. When that energy fails, activity ceases. For example, many toys operate on batteries. Dead batteries bring the toys to a quick halt. Nothing in creation is self-sufficient. Living things in our world must be constantly energized. God is the source of all energy and the master preserver of all things. First He created; now He daily sustains. Paul reminded us that in God "all things hold together" (Col. 1:17).

NOTHING IN CREATION IS SELF-SUFFICIENT.

While the Spirit works in our physical world, His primary interest focuses on our spiritual world. In this realm He works to restore and maintain fellowship with the Father. Jesus said of the Spirit, "He will testify about me" (John 15:26). That is an important work of the Holy Spirit—to testify to the world about the life, ministry, and salvation plan of Christ. For this reason, Christ called Him "the Spirit of truth." He tells us about the One who is "the truth" in 14:6: "Jesus answered, 'I am the way and the truth and the life. No one comes to the Father except through me.'"

Jesus said when the Spirit comes to our world He will bring conviction to sinners, urge people to live righteous lives, and warn of the coming judgment (16:8). These three tasks summarize the Spirit's work in the lives of prebelievers. We call it "prevenient grace," which actually means *the grace that goes before.* Prevenient grace encompasses all that God graciously does before we get saved to bring us to the point of salvation.

Most people think of "finding God" or "getting religion" like a game of hide-and-seek. God hides and dares us to find

Him. If we can locate Him by going to church, talking to a religious friend, or reading a Bible, He will save us. This analogy fails for two important reasons. First, we have neither the desire nor the means to initiate a search for God. Left to ourselves, we couldn't care less whether or not we know God. Second, God does not hide from us; He does everything within His power to reveal himself to us.

A better picture is that of the Spirit taking the initiative of a hound and seeking us out. I remember as a child on the farm watching our neighbor's hounds tirelessly sniffing for an opossum or a raccoon. Once they picked up the trail, they followed it through field and forest until they treed the animal. Then they stood at the base of the tree barking for their master to come. In that same way, God takes the initiative in searching for us. He reasons and pleads with us. He makes us an offer we ought not to refuse. He won't leave us alone until we understand the terms and at least consider His offer of salvation. If we refuse, He keeps coming back with fresh appeals to try and convince us to accept Him.

How does the Spirit make His offer of salvation to those who do not know or acknowledge God? Sometimes we hear Him in our conscience warning us against a course of action. Sometimes He speaks through a pastor or Christian friend or parent giving us sound advice. Sometimes the circumstances of life come at us in such ways that our thoughts turn to God. Sometimes our plans to do wrong fail and our best efforts at having our own way collapse. Sometimes we are left dry and unsatisfied by the choices we make in life.

Mere circumstances? No. These and a thousand others become the Spirit's means of making us stop and pay attention to Him. Usually He works quietly behind the scenes of our lives, but He works nonetheless.

Why talk about this aspect of the Spirit's work with readers who probably already have a relationship with Him? First, it reminds us of all God does to bring us to himself and establish or restore relationship. Second, it encourages us to continue to pray for our lost friends and loved ones. For some mysterious reason, God's prevenient grace works more effectively in the lives of people on our prayer lists. So, pray on. God hasn't given up on our lost friends, and neither should we.

# DAY 11

**Remember:**

The Spirit of Christ is at work in our world.

*When he comes, he will convict the world of guilt in regard to sin and righteousness and judgment* (John 16:8).

# A GUIDE FOR YOU

*But when he, the Spirit of truth, comes, he will guide you into all truth* (John 16:13).

WHAT DOES the Spirit do in the hearts and lives of those who choose to accept and follow Christ? That's a tough question. It's not tough because it's hard to find evidence of His work. It's tough because He works so pervasively in the hearts and lives of believers that it's hard to find anything He does not affect. Today I will suggest a few areas of the Spirit's involvement; it's not exhaustive or all-inclusive. Your own personal testimony will, no doubt, remind you of several other ways the Spirit has worked in your life.

1. The Spirit gives us new birth and faith in God (John 3:3-6). The Spirit draws us to God and gives us this incredible new birth. Your new birth has made you a new creature in Christ.

2. Once you become a Christian, He lives in your heart and illuminates your mind to the things of God (John 14:16-17). He gives you spiritual eyes to begin to see things as God sees them and value as God values. Over a period of time you develop what the Bible calls "the mind of Christ" (1 Cor. 2:16).

3. He inspires your mind when you read the Bible and guides you to truth (John 16:13). The Spirit of God enlivens the Word of God and makes it a living message

to your soul. When you read the Bible, the Spirit of God speaks directly to you. He both teaches you new spiritual truth and reminds you of forgotten truths.

4. He brings you the presence of the living Christ (John 16:15-16). This is the specific work of the Spirit that earns Him the name "the Spirit of Christ." Notice the last portion of verse 16. What do you think Jesus meant when He told His disciples, "after a little while you will see me"? No doubt, Jesus referred to His bodily resurrection with these words. But what about after He returned to the Father? They certainly saw Him again in a spiritual sense with the Spirit's outpouring.

5. He intercedes on your behalf to the Father (Rom. 8:26-27). What a powerful ministry! Paul says, "The Spirit himself intercedes for us" and "the Spirit intercedes for the saints in accordance with God's will." You have a direct line of communication in prayer to the Father through His Spirit.

6. He sanctifies your heart by faith (Rom. 8:1-17).

7. He produces spiritual fruit in your life (Gal. 5:22-23). As you grow in God's grace, the Spirit grows a healthy crop of fruit in you: love, joy, peace, patience, kindness, goodness, faithfulness, gentleness, and self-control.

8. He gives you gifts and abilities for ministry in His church and to His world (Rom. 12; 1 Cor. 12; Eph. 4). We often think of believers using their talents and abilities in the church, but it's far more than natural talent. The Spirit actually gifts believers with abilities for use in the Christian community.

9. He works through the church to win new converts and make disciples. Evangelism doesn't succeed because of skillful planning by those charged with forwarding the cause of Christianity. A good business model does not guarantee positive results. Rather, the Spirit empowers

believers to witness and work in ways that win converts and disciple them.

10. The Spirit's most significant work internalizes God's presence in you. His presence does not remain outside like light in a room. Rather, He internalizes His presence like a pacemaker placed inside your body. God lives within your heart in a way unique to Christianity. Though He fills you, you never hold all of His presence. We have God's presence within us, just as the Prophet Ezekiel foresaw hundreds of years ago, "I will . . . put a new spirit in you" (36:26).

We've looked at the notion of a Spirit guide. Not just any spirit guide—but the very presence of God himself. This discovery ranks as number one because it's essential to all of the remaining discoveries. We will never place emphasis in this study on discovering intellectual concepts disconnected from God's presence. Knowledge of God can never replace relationship with Him. The remaining discoveries of the days that follow are all rooted in your relationship with God. They're all by-products of that relationship, not stand-alone concepts.

So the first discovery on your quest to find the life you've longed for teaches you that the Spirit of Christ offers to be your Spirit Guide. What an extreme thought!

# DAY 12

**Remember:**

The Spirit of Christ wants to indwell and guide you.

*But when he, the Spirit of truth, comes, he will guide you into all truth* (John 16:13).

# DISCOVERY 2
## YOU CAN ACCEPT LOVE.

---

## Memory Verse for the Week

*Love the Lord your God with all your heart and with all your soul and with all your mind and with all your strength. The second is this: Love your neighbor as yourself. There is no commandment greater than these* (Mark 12:30-31).

# LOVE FLOATS

*But the greatest of these is love* (1 Cor. 13:13).

THE FARM on which I grew up lay just across the highway from my grandparents' farm. My grandparents milked dairy cattle twice a day along with growing a variety of grains. I grew up with a gallon of fresh milk in our refrigerator every morning. Of course, that was decades prior to the popular preference for skim milk. This week Sue bought some "extra skim" milk. I think it's just flavored water in a milk jug! Our whole milk from the farm still contained the cream, all of the calories, and plenty of flavor!

I'm amused as an adult when I visit our local grocery store and see pints of what they now call heavy whipping cream. The name might imply cream to be heavier than regular milk. Quite the contrary. Because rich cream is lighter than milk, it floats to the surface.

If we think of putting every Christian virtue, such as self-control, gentleness, faithfulness, goodness, kindness, patience, peace, joy, and love, in a bowl of water, love will float to the very top as the most important Christian virtue of them all. That's the summary message Paul communicated in his analysis found in 1 Cor. 13. He takes a closer look at faith, hope, and love. Read this chapter again. Notice all the things the world places a high price tag on, then note that Paul rates love as the greatest of them all.

Love floats to the surface because it is the most important Christian virtue described in the Bible. Furthermore, love represents a key ingredient in every other Christian virtue. What virtuous quality does God seek for us that does not in some way include an element of love? Love pervades the entire scope of Christian life and character.

## TRUE LOVE TOUCHES REAL PEOPLE

Love. We're quite familiar with the word. We use it throughout the day to express our feelings, attitudes, or preferences for just about everything: hot coffee, a favorite color, hobbies, pets, weather pattern, coworkers, friends, family members, and God. The English word does not serve us well; it references too many attachments. So, let's train our minds to recognize the difference between common, special, and sacred objects of our love.

You probably first heard the word as a baby when your parents told you how much they loved you. You didn't really know what that meant, nor did you care as long as you received regular feedings and dry pants. As you grew older, though, those expressions of love became more valuable to you. You knew what was meant by the word and you craved declarations of love. You still value those expressions of love coming your way.

What is this thing we all value so highly? The greeting card, candy, and floral industries all provide us with a variety of products for expressing love. What is it they help us say? I looked in the dictionary. Once I disqualified "a score of zero in tennis" and feelings toward animals and objects, I found that "love" refers to a strong affection leading to action toward another person often based on admiration, benevolence, or common interests. Love results in attachment, enthusiasm, admiration, or devotion to this person. It usually leads to unselfish loyalty or benevolent concern for the good of this special one.

These definitions speak more of action than feelings. It hones in on a particular individual in the midst of all humanity. It changes us as we embrace a high regard for another person. It leads to loyalty and benevolence. These represent ways we want God and other people to think, feel, and act toward us. It also represents the ways God wants us to think, feel, and act toward Him and others.

This analysis, then, reminds us that love is more than a warm, fuzzy feeling we get when we think about the object of our love. It describes ways of acting toward God and others. I recently attended a meeting where I heard a woman say, "I love poor people." Someone quickly responded, "What are their names?" You see, love is not lofty abstract; it must translate into a practical, concrete gesture aimed toward a person with a name. True love touches real people.

Something deep within you drives you on a quest to find this love that comes from God and others and empowers you to return it to them. You know intuitively that love is the greatest and highest virtue. Where and how do you discover this kind of love? That is the focus of our quest this week.

# DAY 13

## Remember:

All things considered: love floats.

*But the greatest of these is love* (1 Cor. 13:13).

# DAY 14
# GOD = LOVE

*God is love. Whoever lives in love lives in God, and God in him* (1 John 4:16).

WHILE I made my grapefruit juice this morning, I heard a song about God's love. The lyrics attempted to define love, then gave up on the hopeless task and painted a picture. God's love defies definition, even for religious experts. I looked through a few books after breakfast trying to find a comprehensive definition of God's love. All the scholars I read talked around the edges of the subject for several pages, then they all settled on the same picture painted in the song. Next, I turned to the Bible for a definition of God's love. I found numerous descriptors and that same picture again. I'll give you the picture in a minute. For now, let's focus on this indefinable love.

From earliest childhood I heard about God's love. I sang children's songs like "Jesus Loves Me" and "God Is Love" as far back as I can remember. I memorized the most familiar verse in the Bible, "For God so loved the world . . ." (John 3:16). You may have had this same sort of exposure to God's love as well. It's so common to most of us that it loses its mystery. Think for a minute: God does not possess love the way I own a pickup truck. God defines all that we know about love by His very nature and being. He is the source of all love, the very personification of it.

No quest for the love we seek can be thorough without first looking to God and His relationship to it. Biblical images and references abound, telling of God's love for us. He presents himself to us as our Heavenly Father (Exod. 4:22; Deut. 1:31;

32:36). Moses reminded the Hebrew people that everything in the universe belongs to God, yet He has set His affection on us and lavished us with His love (Deut. 10:14-15). The Bible beautifully represents God's love for us in the life example of the prophet Hosea. Read again this Old Testament book named for the prophet; see God's love reaching out individually to those of us who are lost and undesirable.

The most amazing expression of God's love comes in the gospel message of the Father sending His Son Jesus Christ to live among us and tell us personally about God's love. Then He died on the Cross for our sins. Unbelievable love! There's the picture I heard described in the song at breakfast and read about in commentaries and Scripture. When pressed to define God's love, John pointed to a picture, "This is how we know what love is: Jesus Christ laid down his life for us" (1 John 3:16).

HIS LOVE

IS

INFINITE.

This picture reminds us that God's love reached out to us before we even knew we needed Him. He continued to reach out to us again and again, even when we willfully rejected Him and ran from Him. He sacrificed His most precious loved one for us. He found no price too high for our ransom. He offered us hope and a plan for a better life. He cared, gave, and worked for our good long before any of us responded to Him. He did the same for those who never responded. This selfless love always was and forever will remain undeserved by us. Yet, He continues to extend it freely.

Now I know why so few Christian authors attempt to define God's love. It defies adequate description. It's like trying to capture the beauty of a tropical island with paint on canvas. We may sit in silence and ponder it, but we will never fully grasp it. Not now, not later in this life, not in all eternity. God is infinite; His love is infinite. We are finite creatures; we will remain finite creatures forever. Finite can never fully comprehend infinite.

Your assignment for the next million years, should you choose to accept it, is to ponder God's infinite love. You'll never fully grasp it, though it can grasp you. You'll never fully apprehend it, though it can apprehend you. You'll never fully contain it, though it can contain you.

So, here's the map for your quest. Head straight toward a more comprehensive understanding of this God who equals love.

# DAY 14

**Remember:**

God is love; enough said.

*God is love* (1 John 4:16).

DAY 15

# THE GREAT COMMAND

*The most important one is, . . . "Love the Lord your God with all your heart and with all your soul and with all your mind and with all your strength." The second is this: "Love your neighbor as yourself." There is no command- ment greater than these* (Mark 12:30-31).

WE LIVE in a give-it-to-me-quick world. We don't want to sit through a full report of the evening news; give us quick sound bites that summarize the day's events. We don't want to wade through long pages of reports at the office; get to the bot- tom line. We don't want to read a long novel; summarize it in a 90-minute movie. That's the mind-set that prompted one of the teachers of the Law to request Jesus to cut through the thousands of Jewish laws and interpretations thereof to the heart of the matter. In other words, he wanted Jesus to cut to the chase. Jesus did exactly that in today's text.

Jesus replied with a twofold response: love the Lord with all your heart, soul, mind, and strength and your neighbor as yourself. The first command summarizes the first four of the Ten Commandments; the second summarizes the last six. If we love God with all we have within us and others as ourselves, we have realized God's intentions for the Ten Commandments. Love for God must always come first; love for others will natu- rally flow from it.

Jesus did not put forth a new command in His summary.

The Bible highlighted love for God as the primary motivation for serving Him. We do not obey His laws out of slavish obligation but with a child's heart of love. We reverence Him and prefer His ways because we love Him. One of the most profound insights into understanding sin reminds us that sin does not break God's laws as much as it breaks His heart. If we truly love Him, we will not want to intentionally hurt Him.

Look in Deuteronomy. The heart of the book comes in 6:4-5. Especially note verse 5: "Love the LORD your God with all your heart and with all your soul and with all your strength." This call to love God threads its way through the entire book (7:12; 10:12; 11:1, 13, 22; 13:3; 19:9; 30:6, 16, 20). How is it possible for us to love God in this way? He gives us a pattern for love: we are to love God and others the way He first loved us. We find the message of God's love for us scattered throughout Deuteronomy (5:10; 7:9, 13; 33:3). Though many things are uncertain in this world, one is settled and sure. Never doubt God's love for you. Accept it and reach out to love others as you have been loved.

Jesus picked up and strengthened His call to love God and others in His Sermon on the Mount by reminding us to guard the internal motivation for all of our actions. He reminded us that the Father not only sees what we do but also sees what we think and feel. He looks at and judges our hearts as the fountainhead of our actions. The Old Testament said, "Do not murder." Jesus said, "Do not have evil feelings toward others." The Old Testament said, "Do not commit adultery." Jesus said, "Do not harbor lust in your heart." The Old Testament allowed for divorce; Jesus took it out of the discussion, except for marital unfaithfulness. The Old Testament said, "Keep your oaths." Jesus said, "Speak so you do not need oaths." The Old Testament allowed for limited revenge; Jesus said we should not want revenge. The Old Testament said, "Love your neighbor." Jesus said, "Love everyone, even your enemies" (see Matt. 5:21-48).

On another occasion, Jesus summarized the Law and the Prophets (a common reference for Old Testament law) by saying, "In everything, do to others what you would have them do to you" (Matt. 7:12). We call this the Golden Rule. We must always keep the biblical principle of love for God and others at the center of our thinking as we proceed on our quest to discover the life we've longed for.

The apostle John picked up on Jesus' thoughts and developed them further for us. He frequently referred to living a life of love. He said all of our actions should be from a heart of love for God and one another. He discussed love 21 times in his Gospel and 24 times in 1 John. He could hardly discuss any subject without bringing love into it.

Love begins with God, who loved us first. "As the Father has loved me, so have I loved you. Now remain in my love" (John 15:9). It continues with us loving one another. "By this all men will know that you are my disciples, if you love one another" (13:35). Jesus reminded us that we show God that we love Him by obeying His commands (14:15-24). Watch for the love theme as you read John's writings.

The Great Command admonishes us to be sure that we mark everything in our lives with love. We can easily be kind to those who are nice to us; we're not as easily disposed to have that same regard for those who mistreat us. But Jesus gave us that revolutionary charge. Our love responses for God and others create one of the most important characteristics of our Christian faith.

# DAY 15

**Remember:**

Love God, love others. That's it.

*Love the Lord your God . . . love your neighbor* (Mark 12:30-31).

# DAY 16
# IMITATORS OF GOD

*Be imitators of God, therefore, as dearly loved children, and live a life of love, just as Christ loved us and gave himself up for us as a fragrant offering and sacrifice to God* (Eph. 5:1-2).

ONE OF MY favorite memories of Brent's childhood occurred during the summer of his third year. One hot day while mowing the yard, I saw something out of the corner of my eye that taught me an important lesson about parenting. There Brent was about three paces behind me pushing his toy mower, imitating every move I made. He didn't stop when I saw him. Rather, he proudly displayed the fact that he could do everything I was doing. He might be small, but he could perform grown-up tasks. I never forgot that object lesson. Like it or not, our kids imitate what they see us do. It's natural for children to imitate their parents, and not just when they are small. It becomes a life pattern.

That's the concept Paul had in mind when he admonished us in our text to imitate God. Sounds like a tall order, doesn't it? Paul didn't leave us guessing about what he wanted us to do. In the verse just prior to our text, he said, "Be kind and compassionate to one another, forgiving each other" (4:32).

Paul also didn't leave us guessing as to how he expected us to fill his tall order. Both 4:32 and 5:2 provide a pattern to follow. Both verses say we do it just as Christ did it. We imitate

Him. He's already been kind and compassionate toward us. He's already lived a life of love before us. He's already given himself for us in death as our sacrifice. Now, we are to imitate His attitude and lifestyle the way we saw Him do it. We follow His example and show others the same kindness and compassion we have received from Him. He took His example to its ultimate extreme in dying for us. Few of us will be called upon to express our love for another person or God to the point of death. However, if it comes to that, we're willing. We will simply follow His example.

What force drives this love? It's not supersized affection; it's not blind emotion. Rather, God's love *flows* through us. This love we share with others does not belong to us nor does it find its source in us. This love originates in God. We simply receive it and pass it on to our hurting world. It contains no mixture of selfish ambition for personal advancement. We strive to love others the way the Father loves His Son and the way the Son loves us. That love won't go unnoticed in our love-hungry world. It can't. We become channels through whom His love flows. This explains our ability to love our enemies and those who frustrate or oppose us. We love them with a love God gives us. We love them the way Christ loves them and us.

Allow me to throw in a quick warning: loving God's way can hurt. It's not all candy hearts and red roses. It cost the Father His Son; it brought the Son death on a cross. Loving God's way is often misunderstood by others, even by the recipients of your love. Imitating God won't always be easy. Sometimes it will cut you to the depths of your heart. It's during those dark nights of the soul, when love is costing you dearly, that you remind yourself that you are loving those hardest to love with a love God gives you.

One of my favorite illustrations of loving others with God's love comes from the Early Church. In the early days of Christianity, ministers compared our hearts to a mirror. Sin makes the mirror dirty and unusable. Christ forgives our sins and thus cleans the mirror of our hearts. Now we can aim our reflective mirrors toward God. When others look at our lives, they see the mirror image of God in us. It's not just a static image like a painting on the wall. Rather, our mirrors give us the ability to receive God's love and then become a channel through whom God flows to love others. He uses our words and deeds to reach out to hurting people around us. Isn't that a wonderful illustration?

## IT'S NOT ALL CANDY HEARTS AND RED ROSES

In the Bible lesson for today, love becomes more than affection; it's a principle of life that leads to action. As John reminds us, "Dear children, let us not love with words or tongue but with actions and in truth" (1 John 3:18). We've talked about our love for poor people translating into actual names. True love touches real people. John reminds us that our words must become deeds.

Yesterday we were reminded that our love for God must exceed our love for everything else. It must show forth in our actions. This resolve means that whenever we see something else taking center stage in our lives, we quickly set it aside and restore God to first place. We also begin to see people as God sees them. We genuinely care about their needs and seek to find ways to meet those needs. Again, our care shows in our actions. We don't just have sympathetic thoughts about those needs; we translate sympathy into deeds. That's where the text for today's study finds reality in action. Because God has reached out to you in love in ways you have experienced, you reach out to others with that same love.

Paul's admonition in today's study adds direction to your quest. This week's discovery reminds you that you can accept love for the life you long for. Where's the love you're accepting?

God's love. It's such a simple act, but I cannot overestimate its importance. So often when Christians read in the Bible that they must love God and others, they assume they must generate large quantities of this love by themselves. So, like the car rental employee, they try harder. And, they try. And, they try. Then they become frustrated, because they cannot love God's way by themselves. Trying harder will never work. The love you're called to display requires nothing more than your reflection of God's love passed on to others. You simply imitate our God.

# DAY 16

**Remember:**

Imitate God.

*Be imitators of God* (Eph. 5:1).

# A GOLDEN RULE

*So in everything, do to others what you would have them do to you, for this sums up the Law and the Prophets* (Matt. 7:12).

OUR STUDIES this week have narrowed our focus from noting the importance of love, to recognizing God as the source and author of love, to hearing His command for us to love Him and others with both words and deeds, and finally to finding ourselves as channels of His love as we reflect it to others. Let's narrow our focus a bit more as we hear Jesus' words again reminding us of how this love looks in daily life.

We call it the Golden Rule for a couple of reasons. First, like valuable gold, Jesus placed it at the top of the list of most important things He said during His earthly ministry. Second, following this rule results in the best kind of life we can live. Let's look closer at what Jesus says here.

Our Scripture verse begins with "so" or "therefore." When you see the word "so" in the NIV and "therefore" in the KJV and NASB, they signal a radical new thought from Jesus. The common wisdom of the day urged people to avoid doing harm to others. The rabbinic Jewish tradition, as well as world religions like Hinduism, Buddhism, and Confucianism, all urge us to: "Do no harm to others." Jesus stands that thought on its head, reversing it into a positive command. Treat others with the same acts of kindness and goodwill that you would enjoy receiving.

In other words, pursue joy and happiness for others. Think of the kind of party you would like to have, then plan it for someone else. Think of a really nice gift, then buy it for a friend. Include those who frustrate and aggravate you on your list of possible recipients. Don't forget to put your enemies on that list as well.

Everyone can love in this way. You don't need a college education to understand or apply it. You don't need a certain income level or social status to employ it. It doesn't take a great deal of thought or tedious practice to perfect it. No one disagrees about its importance. People do not get mad at you for applying the rule to them. It works in every circumstance of life and needs no adjustment for specialized situations. It's a one-size-fits-all rule for displaying love.

Think for a minute about all of the areas of life where you can use this rule. As I name a few areas below, think how you would apply this Golden Rule to everyday situations with family members, friends, church acquaintances, irritating workmates, pesky neighbors, and outright enemies.

- Your actions toward them.
- Your lack of action toward them.
- Your reactions to them.
- Your attitude about them.
- Judgments you form of them.
- Your speech to them.
- Your offhand comments to them.
- Your offhand comments about them.
- Your business dealings with them.
- Your leisure time with them.
- Your community service for them.

Jesus did not give us the Golden Rule for us to follow like a military command or a civil law. He gave us the example of His own life, actions, reactions, judgments, attitudes, speech, business dealings, and all the rest. He urged us to trace His movements the way we lay tracing paper over a picture and copy it.

Jesus not only gave us an example for following the Golden Rule but also gave us the inspiration to follow it. He called us to a life that leads to peace and harmony in our relationships with others. He called us to a life of wholeness with this rule.

Along with an example and inspiration, Jesus further gave us the strength and power to follow this Golden Rule. All this week we have emphasized the fact that this love for which we quest does not find its source in us. It flows from God himself. That's why we must constantly remind ourselves that it's not ours to produce; it's ours to receive. We must accept this gift of love from God then pass it along in the same measure in which we have received it.

On the surface, the Golden Rule described in today's Bible verse sounds impossible to put into practice on a daily basis. Yes, it is quite impossible under your own power. Possibilities for its fulfillment in your life materialize only as you live in close personal relationship with God through the Spirit of Christ living within you. It's interesting, isn't it, how your quest keeps bringing you back to the need of a close personal relationship with God? The more you travel on your quest, the more you keep coming back to this relationship.

# Day 17

**Remember:**
Apply the Golden Rule to everything you say and do every day with everyone.

*Do to others what you would have them do to you* (Matt. 7:12).

# LOVE'S NOT ALWAYS EASY

*But we have this treasure in jars of clay to show that this all-surpassing power is from God and not from us (2 Cor. 4:7).*

LOVING GOD and others sounds manageable as we begin our Christian walk. It gets a little tough, however, as we begin to interact with people who are a bit hard to love. Young believers sometimes become discouraged and even disillusioned when they come face-to-face with the startling realization that even the saints at church remain fully human. They're sometimes as hard to love as sinners in the world. What's that all about?

But then, one look in the mirror provides a reality check that reminds us of our own imperfections. If we're honest with ourselves, we see our own shortcomings and weak spots. We realize that God cuts each of us a great deal of slack with His grace and mercy. His grace blesses us in ways we do not deserve; His mercy withholds from us corrections we deserve. We are ever mindful of and thankful for God's undeserved grace and mercy.

Here's where imitating God comes in again. As we become more like Him, we extend to others the same grace and mercy we have received from God. By doing this, we come to terms with the less than perfect condition of others. We recognize our brothers and sisters in Christ as "saints in the making."

In 2 Cor. 4:6 Paul says, "For God, who said, 'Let light shine

81

out of darkness,' made his light shine in our hearts to give us the light of the knowledge of the glory of God in the face of Christ." We enjoy the benefits of that light daily. Paul compares this event to the time when God brought new light to the world by sending His Son, Jesus. We enjoy the spiritual benefits of that light in our lives today. Verse 7 tells us, "We have this treasure in jars of clay to show that this all-surpassing power is from God and not from us." We carry that treasure in our jars of clay, that is, in our humanity.

NONE OF US LIVES IN A PERFECT OR STRESS-FREE ENVIRONMENT.

In biblical times the wealthy used jars of clay to hide valuables in their homes. Thieves didn't expect to find expensive jewelry or money in worthless clay pots on a hallway shelf. In this same way, God has placed His valuable message of salvation with humans. The power of God's love at work in our lives far exceeds surface appearances. When others look at our lives, they realize an unexplainable power works in us. We realize this power comes from God. We're simply reflecting God's love to those around us. We remain completely humble and dependent upon Him. He deserves the credit for all good things accomplished in our lives.

In verses 8 and 9 of this passage Paul describes the condition in which he finds himself. Life is not easy for him. He is "hard pressed on every side, but not crushed; perplexed, but not in despair; persecuted, but not abandoned; struck down, but not destroyed." Paul describes the stresses and pressure he feels pressing in from every direction.

The literal meaning of verse 8 contains a play on words: "being at a loss, but not utterly at a loss." Paul feels the sharp sword of persecution and feels struck to the ground like a soldier knocked down in battle. He identifies with Christ not only in His suffering but also in His dying. He willingly submits to all of these difficulties because of his total identification with the cause of Christ and personal commitment to Him. Paul states his mind-set clearly in 2 Tim. 2:11, "If we died with him, we will also live with him."

This passage of Scripture reminds us that none of us lives in a perfect or stress-free environment. Loving others as God calls us to love would be simple if we lived in Easyville. We could just read our Bibles and pray as we sip coffee by the fire. However, we don't live in a perfect world. We feel the pressures and stresses of life in their varied forms. We live with schedules that often seem beyond our control. Sometimes the children simply won't cooperate with our plans. Add to that the normal mood swings we humans experience. Add to that the aches and pains of our physical bodies. Add to that the variety of personality types represented. What do we have? A formula for less-than-perfect saints acting and reacting in less-than-perfect ways! Less-than-perfect saints—not to mention outright sinners—can be mighty hard to love sometimes.

On the days you feel stressed by circumstances and irritating people, acknowledge the fact that it's not going to be easy for you to love them. Just simply admit the obvious. Then remind yourself of all the ways God's grace and mercy work in your life. Never forget the fragile nature of jars of clay—your own or your fellow brothers and sisters in Christ. That's where you can extend to others the same grace and mercy that God extends to you on a daily basis. That makes love easier. Jesus illustrated this with a powerful parable about a man forgiven of a great debt. Read it again in Matt. 18:23-34 and apply it to your life.

A story from the lives of Peter and Paul illustrates an important reminder: saints remain human. Gal. 2:11-14 recounts the story. Even believers continue to live with their human natures;

they still must use free will wisely every day. They face temptation. They have blind spots and prejudices. They lack insight and understanding about certain areas of life. They have unique personalities. They continue to deal with areas of immaturity, they still have human frailties and weaknesses. In no way do these realities diminish the grace and mercy of God at work in believers' lives. Nor do they depreciate God's plan of salvation in our lives or His work among us. However, if we fail to take the human element into account as we live together in the Christian community, we set ourselves up for certain disappointment.

In this Bible story, Peter displayed prejudices against fellow believers. Paul recognized these prejudices were wrong and called Peter's hand on them. Peter, no doubt, accepted the correction and adjusted his behaviors and attitudes. They continued their fellowship as brothers in faith. This story illustrates the fragile nature of our jars of clay and the way Christian love works in stressful situations. It reminds us of the importance of cutting one another slack in the same manner in which God's grace cuts us slack. It's all about imitating God when we realize that love is not always easy to give to both sinners and saints.

# DAY 18

**Remember:**

It's not always easy to love; God can show us the way.

*But we have this treasure in jars of clay to show that this all-surpassing power is from God and not from us* (2 Cor. 4:7).

# IS THIS THING FOR REAL?

*How great is the love the Father has lavished on us, that we should be called children of God! And that is what we are!* (1 John 3:1).

WE'VE BEEN looking this week at the virtue of love. No one has to tell us that it's a good thing; we know that. No one has to tell us that we need it or that we should give it to others; we know that too. It's as if God hardwired us to place high importance on it. The entertainment industry understands this, devoting movies and music to portraying love's value.

We often refer to love as a Christian quality, yet religions, philosophies, and societies the world over value it supremely. Nations and cultures that value hate, antipathy, animosity, and hostility do not survive for long; they disintegrate quickly. Chaos reigns. Innocent victims get hurt. People die. Watch the video footage of war, crime, acts of hatred, and depreciation of human life on the news tonight. Hate paints a dark picture.

But in spite of all of the attention love receives from world religions, secular society, and the entertainment sector, our hearts long for something more. This longing takes us on a quest to find a deeper kind of love. This is the love we hunger for but don't find in the world in general. What we're searching for can only be found in Christian love.

Christian love comes from God, the source of all love. Only through knowing Him and living in relationship with Him can we find love for the life we long for. The Bible speaks often about God's love without giving much of a definition for love. But is it really necessary for the Bible to tell us what love should be? We know. We just don't know where to find it. Then the Bible gives us this incredible picture of God's love. It is the picture of Jesus dying on the Cross for us. What a powerful statement, "This is how we know what love is: Jesus Christ laid down his life for us" (1 John 3:16).

So, our quest for true love points us back to God. Now what? Are we to see God's love in action and just decide that we will do likewise? You might assume as much from the great command of Jesus we studied on Day 15. When He summarized the message of the entire Old Testament, He challenged us to love God with all of our hearts, souls, minds, and strength and our neighbors as ourselves. It's simple enough to toss the challenge out, but can we love in that way just by willing it? I'm afraid it's not that easy. Even with determined willpower, we fall short every time.

The Bible tells us we must first accept the fact that God reaches out and loves us. We must accept His love for us. Once we accept His love, we can turn around and love others the way He loved us. We must first imitate God's manner and pattern of loving by following His example—the way a daughter imitates her mom in the kitchen as she learns to bake cookies.

It doesn't take long to realize that God's love cannot be imitated by our own abilities, no matter how hard we try. That's where Christian love comes to the rescue. Christian love is not a love we generate from within by determined willing or imagination. Rather, it speaks of God flowing through us to love others. We become channels through whom He works to reach out with loving acts of kindness and goodness. We do not create Christian love; we simply dispense it as a gift. That's the same way we received it—a gift straight from God.

Our discovery for this week urges us to accept God's love. It's easy to love those who love us. It's easy to be nice to those who admire us. It's even easy to say we love our enemies. The love we're talking about this week—God's love—reaches far beyond mutual admiration, sentiment, or lofty speech. It is daily action toward both friend and foe. In fact, Jesus urges us to do a seemingly strange thing. Sit down and imagine how you would most like to be treated, then treat others that way. That puts a new spin on things, doesn't it?

Like the telemarketers say, "But wait; there's more." Jesus goes even further and urges us to do these nice things not only for friends and loved ones but also for those who frustrate and aggravate us, as well as for our enemies. Now that's a really new spin! Does it sound impossible? It is—by our own strength. Only God flowing through us changes us and allows us to love in that way.

It may be tempting to dismiss the ideal of Christian love as unrealistic. However, remember that God places His love in us the same way He gives us salvation. Remember the light in the clay pots we discussed yesterday. If you can accept the miracle and mystery of His salvation, you can also accept the miracle and mystery of His love. Receive it; pass it on. It's that simple.

When your neighbors get on your nerves, ask God to help you love them with God's love. When your coworkers steal your good ideas and take credit for them, ask God to help you love them with God's love. When your enemies tell lies about you and try to ruin your good name . . . you get the drill.

I'm not just talking about hypotheticals; I'm giving you a glimpse into my personal life. You see, I know how a friend's betrayal feels. I know about half-truths told in an attempt to tarnish your good name. I know the hurt of someone taking my good intentions and twisting them into evil. When those situations arose in my life, my human nature did not naturally equip me with a tendency to respond with love to those who meant me harm. In those situations, I can personally testify that God's gift of love flowed through me to repay with God's good those who intended to harm me. Don't ask me how He did it. I can't explain it. I just know God's love is for real. He can work through you in the darkest valleys of your journey.

Think about this week's discovery and internalize it. Accept God's love, then live the life you've longed for. The answer to the question in today's title is yes, this thing is for real!

# DAY 19

**Remember:**

God's love is for real.

*How great is the love the Father has lavished on us, that we should be called children of God! And that is what we are!* (1 John 3:1).

# DISCOVERY 3
## YOU CAN EXPERIENCE PURITY.

—

## Memory Verse for the Week

*Blessed are the pure in heart,*
*for they will see God* (Matt. 5:8).

# NOT ANOTHER LECTURE

*Now that you have purified yourselves by obeying the truth so that you have sincere love for your brothers, love one another deeply, from the heart* (1 Pet. 1:22).

WHEN I was a child, I remember my dad coming home for supper after spending the day working in the fields on a tractor or combine. He talked at the top of his voice for an hour or so; we responded by shouting our responses back to him until his hearing returned to normal. His ears were exposed to the loud roar of the farm machinery for so many hours that they no longer responded to normal sounds.

The next quest takes us in the direction of seeking purity for the life we've longed for. I know as soon as some people read about a search for purity they grip their seats in preparation for another lecture. Teens expect to hear about sexual purity and good dating practices. "Don't do this; don't go there." Young adults expect to hear about making wise choices regarding entertainment and lifestyle. "Don't watch this; don't drink that." Older adults expect to hear another lecture on performing good deeds or not falling into sin. "Go to church more; watch that attitude."

When purity is the topic, many people put up their defenses. In fact, some folks unconsciously build up enough resistance to go somewhat deaf, the way my dad did after a long day on the tractor. Only it's the type of deafness that afflicts teens when Mom tells them to clean their bedrooms.

Relax; I'm not going to throw a guilt ball at you. Neither am I going to ask you to answer a list of personal questions or rate yourself on a scale from 1 to 10 about your lifestyle choices or dating practices. I am going to point you in the direction of the Bible to explore what it has to say about purity. As disciples of Jesus Christ, we feel drawn on a quest for purity. We know it's a Christian virtue, but we don't always have a biblical understanding of it. Our quest this week explores biblical images and stories that direct our thinking toward God's views on purity and His will for our lives.

WE FEEL DRAWN ON A QUEST FOR PURITY.

Let's look at this concept with fresh eyes. We can become so influenced by culture that the biblical meaning of purity loses its strength. Let me illustrate. Last spring I bought a large bag of grass seed to plant in my yard. The tag sown into the top of the bag intrigued me. It read, "Purity rating: 90%." That meant that I could expect 10 percent of the product in the bag to be something other than grass seed. Trash, weed seed, and other impurities worked their way into the bag with the grass seed. The seed producer gave me fair warning that I could expect less than total purity with my bag of seed. I lowered my purity expectations of the product by 10 percent.

Without realizing it, we make that same adjustment in our thinking throughout a normal day of living. Take a minute and think of the many ways society urges us to lower our expectations of people and lifestyle choices.

"Nobody's perfect."

"You should expect me to get angry. I have red hair."

"Kids will be kids."

"Men have a weakness for that, you know."

"He can't help himself; he comes from a dysfunctional family."

"What do you expect? Her mother is an alcoholic."

"So I call in sick when I'm not. I work hard most of the time."

"Everybody fudges on the truth once in a while."

"It can't be that bad; everybody does it."

On and on grows the list of reasons or excuses for less than desirable behavior. Over a period of time we unconsciously lower our expectations until we lose sight of God's intentions or goals for His children. The roar of excuses dulls our hearing, just like the roar of the tractor affected my dad's hearing. Once our ears lose their sensitivity to sound, we quit expecting as much as we once did.

All the excuses in the world, however, don't keep our hearts from longing and searching for purity. God placed that longing deep within us when He created us. Like the need for a spiritual guide and the hunger for love we explored in the previous two quests, our hearts tell us God has something more than the world wants us to believe we should expect.

In our Bible reading for today, we see our previous two discoveries linked to our new one for this week. The verse begins by telling us that we are purified by obeying the truth. The Spirit of Christ, who is the Spirit of Truth, brought us an understanding of His truth. The verse goes on to urge us to use the love God gives us to love others deeply. Peter makes a worthwhile connection between truth, love, and purity.

As you explore the Scriptures this week, keep your defenses down and let God teach you new insights into the biblical notion of purity. Its meaning may be far richer than you imagine. As you read and think about purity, notice how the Bible defines and describes it. Notice, too, that God expects us to live a life of purity in this sin-soaked world. Also, as you read and think this week, get in touch with the inner desire for purity God has placed within you. Enter this week's quest with a new enthusiasm to discover God's dream of purity for His children.

---

# DAY 20

**Remember:**

God's call to purity is not another guilt ball for you to catch. It's a call to obey God's truth.

*Now that you have purified yourselves* . . . (1 Pet. 1:22).

# TO WILL ONE THING

*When Abram was ninety-nine years old, the LORD appeared to him and said, "I am God Almighty; walk before me and be blameless"* (Gen. 17:1).

YESTERDAY I talked about the purity rating of 90 percent for the sack of grass seed I bought. A sack of 100 percent pure grass seed contains only grass seed. No trash. No weed seed. That offers an insight into the biblical understanding of purity.

Purity is not so much perfect performance as it is pure intentions and undivided loyalty. That is the reasoning behind Danish philosopher Søren Kierkegaard's book, *Purity of the Heart Is to Will One Thing.* It speaks to a single purpose in serving God.

A large part of today's society—including many Christians —suffers with fractured attentions and divided loyalty. We all either know or are people who want a fulfilling job and a nice house and a well-manicured lawn and a new car or SUV and a good golf game and well-behaved children and a happy mate, and . . . and . . . Believers and unbelievers alike strive to complete their lists of must-haves. Believers then add a plethora of church roles, activities, and responsibilities. What a staggering expectation!

How on earth can you will just one thing? You can't! Your loyalties are too divided to allow you to focus on purity of direction for life. That's one of the reasons it is important for you to study your purpose. Once you determine God's purpose for your life, you can filter the ambition, activities, and goals of every day through His purpose and see how they measure up. When your list matches His list, you're ready to go. Everything else can go in the trash.

Many of my friends focused their energies on fewer activities once they came to terms with God's purpose for their lives. Their previous activities were not wrong or evil. They simply didn't measure up when examined from God's perspective.

I use this filtering exercise in my job at the university almost every day. I constantly receive letters and e-mails wanting the university to offer a particular course or program of study. I'm told, "You need to add a class in digital photography." Or, "You need to offer an engineering major." People want us to buy property across the street from the university or send a sports team to play in Chicago. Most of these ideas have merit. Merit, however, is not enough. I keep a copy of the university's mission and strategic plan on my desk. I filter every request through that mission and strategic plan. If the request passes that test, I look for ways to make it happen. If it fails the test, I politely decline. Failure to perform that exercise would put our university on 100 different paths with no unifying purpose. We'd be offering more courses with less purpose.

There is a biblical example that illustrates this truth. Gen. 12 begins the story of Abraham. He was a man who followed and pleased God. To this very day, Abraham's life shines as a beacon of direction, showing us how to live a life that pleases God. In Isa. 41:8, God calls Abraham "my friend." God doesn't pass out compliments like that every day.

Abraham and his extended family first lived in Ur, a large city on the southeast side of the Arabian Desert near the Persian Gulf. Idolatry consumed the city, making God's worshipers feel out of place. So Terah, Abraham's father, moved his family far north to the city of Haran where they lived until Terah died. He got them away from the center of idolatry, but he didn't go all the way in getting his family completely out of the land. Terah's move wasn't complete enough for God. So, God gave Abraham a plan to move completely out of his comfort zone to a new land. He promised to bless Abraham, to make him into a great nation, and to bless those who blessed him.

Why did God select Abraham for this special assignment and blessing? The Bible doesn't indicate any unique qualities that gave Abraham an advantage over everyone else on earth. God's special blessing on Abraham reminds us of the way He dispenses His grace. He simply chose to do something special for Abraham and his offspring. It appears that Abraham's only unique quality was his focused faith in God. Rom. 4:3 says, "Abraham believed God, and it was credited to him as righteousness."

BLAMELESS DOES NOT IMPLY PERFECT PERFORMANCE

As you read the life history of Abraham in the Book of Genesis, note how he:

- gave up everything to follow God's call
- moved first to Haran
- then moved again toward God's land of promise
- waited patiently for God to give him the land of promise
- made mistakes
- endured hardships
- waited patiently for God to give him a son
- experienced trials and tests
- and waited patiently for God's spiritual blessing on him and his family

Gen. 17:1 contains God's call to Abraham that interests us particularly in a study of single-mindedness. God says to Abraham, "Walk before me and be blameless." Blameless. That's a powerful notion. The word appears frequently in Paul's New Testament letters, as it does in Phil. 2:15 and 1 Thess. 3:13; 5:23.

Blameless does not imply perfect performance, as in free from mistakes. It pictures a person wholeheartedly seeking to do God's will. There's no mix of wanting God's will along with my will. It's an undiluted desire to do what God wants me to do. God finds such unmixed desire acceptable and characterizes such a life as blameless. The use of the word "blameless" offers another insight into the biblical understanding of purity.

Abraham wasn't perfect. He made his share of mistakes in life. He lied to the Egyptian Pharaoh about Sarah being his wife (Gen. 12:19). He and Sarah got ahead of God and frustrated God's plan for a child by using Hagar as a surrogate mother (16:3). But, through his occasional errors in judgment, Abraham kept fellowship with God, and he sought wholeheartedly to find and do God's will. He willed one thing, as Kierkegaard said. When he stumbled, he sought God's guidance, got back up, and started again.

Single-mindedness cannot stand alone as the sole meaning for purity. However, it illustrates an important insight into God's truth. My new computer recently taught me a lesson about focus. I'd heard only good reports about a particular model. Since my old computer had given me fits for years, I decided to upgrade. I had great expectations of flawless computing with my new machine. I couldn't have been more disappointed! The new one ran slower and caused me more problems than my old one had.

After weeks of frustration, I called a computer technician to come and troubleshoot my new computer. He made an amazing discovery. A factory-generated renegade program consumed 99 percent of the computer's operating power. I was trying to operate with 1 percent of the computer's ability. Once that was corrected, the machine ran great. What does this illustrate for your life?

Remember, for both Abraham and Kierkegaard, the one thing they each willed wasn't his own carefully selected purpose; each sought to find and do God's will.

# DAY 21

**Remember:**

Purity sometimes means simply willing one thing—God's will.

*Walk before me and be blameless* (Gen. 17:1).

# DAY 22
# BURN IT UP!

*Then one of the seraphs flew to me with a live coal in his hand, which he had taken with tongs from the altar. With it he touched my mouth and said, "See, this has touched your lips; your guilt is taken away and your sin atoned for"* (Isa. 6:6-7).

DURING my first year in seminary I worked at a medical center just down the street from the campus. One of my responsibilities at the hospital was sterilizing surgical instruments used in the operating rooms. These instruments came to me washed and rolled in green cloths. I placed a special tape on the rolls that changed color when it reached a certain temperature for a certain period of time. Then I laid the rolls in a special machine and started the sterilization process. I followed strict quality-control procedures; one mistake could endanger a patient's life.

That responsibility taught me an important lesson about purity. High temperatures for an extended period of time kill all that contaminates. That's why the Bible uses fire as a symbol for purity. An early example of this occurred in Moses' life. In Exod. 3:1-6 we find Moses minding his own business as he led a flock of sheep across the hot desert. I doubt Moses sought a special appearance from God on the day God visited him. I think God initiated this special encounter.

When Moses first saw the burning bush, he wasn't impressed. Bushes often ignited on the scorching desert floor. Another day, another burning bush. What caught Moses' attention was that the fire did not consume the bush. Like the bunny we've come to know, it just kept going and going. God used the burning bush to get Moses' attention. Then He used it as an object lesson to emphasize His holiness and purity. Moses responded by removing his sandals to demonstrate respect, humility, and worship. This early biblical use of fire reminds us of fire's symbolic significance for purity.

Another biblical narrative that uses fire to symbolize purity is found in Isa. 6:1-7. The last portion of that passage appears at the beginning of this chapter. Here we find Isaiah, a godly minister, disillusioned and discouraged. His hero and friend, King Uzziah, has just died. The nation has slipped into leadership transition. Isaiah went through the motions of leading a worship service at the Temple. Then, something special happened—God intervened. What Isaiah experienced that day changed his life forever.

Isaiah caught a glimpse of the holiness of God unlike anything he'd seen before. He had attended many meaningful worship services and sensed the presence of God, but nothing like this! Isaiah was amazed as he saw the holy radiance of God. When he saw how holy and spotless God appeared, he immediately looked at himself. He did not like what he saw; he didn't measure up. He needed something in his life that his religion had not given him to this point. Once he caught this brief glimpse of Holy God, he could never be satisfied with remaining the same.

Notice God's use of fire and its purifying properties. And notice how Isaiah's close encounter with the presence of Holy God transformed him. What an example for us! A glimpse of God, even a brief glimpse, raises the bar for us.

It almost always happens like this in the Bible. Moses and Isaiah did not have an encounter with an awesome concept in a book or a startling realization as they participated in mental gymnastics. Both had a real encounter with our living God. In the give and take of that relationship, God revealed new truth to both men. And in both cases, God used fire to make His point.

This reminds me that our quest will never take us far from relationship with the living God. Books offer great truths, and mental exercises deliver impressive insights, but only a relationship with God leads to true discovery. I love to read books about the great truths of God, and I love to have conversations with Christian friends about the ways God deals with us. However, no amount of reading or discussion replaces the value of heart-to-heart contact with God.

Our hearts draw us toward purity. We ask ourselves, "Where can I experience the purity for the life I've longed for?" Today's Bible lessons remind us: God is the source of purity. Only His fire can truly purify our hearts.

We discussed on Day 5 the fulfillment of Jesus' Mount of Olives promise to His disciples. The Spirit came upon them in ways they could not doubt. They talked about that day for the rest of their lives. We know, because when a council meeting of the Christian Church convened 20 years later in Jerusalem, Peter recounted again what the Spirit did in their hearts on the Day of Pentecost as well as what He did in the hearts of Gentiles whom He later filled with His Spirit (Acts 15:1-21).

Imagine that. Twenty years later the disciples still pointed back to a decisive work of God in their hearts on one particular day. By the time of the Jerusalem Council, the Church had spread far beyond the boundaries of Jerusalem, Israel, and the Middle East. It gained strength in established congregations across the Roman Empire and maintained unrestrained growth and expansion.

The Christian Church no longer consisted of Jews alone as it had in the early days of its existence. Countless Gentiles also called themselves Christians as well. Peter, speaking to the Jerusalem Council, added a new thought to what happened when they were filled with the Spirit. To the idea of being filled with power from God (Acts 1:8), Peter said the Spirit also "purified their hearts by faith" (15:9). Remember the second symbol on the Day of Pentecost? Fire. So, we see again, God used His fire to bring purity.

Each day this week we have added a new dimension to a biblical understanding of purity. It involves obeying God's truth, willing one thing—God's will, and encountering God's fire. We'll add to our list tomorrow. Take time today to contemplate the need for God's fire in your life. What might He want to purge from your heart? What might He want to burn out of your life? Let Moses and Isaiah motivate you to open yourself to His purging fire today.

# DAY 22

**Remember:**

God's fire brings purity.

*With it he touched my mouth and said, "See, this has touched your lips; your guilt is taken away and your sin atoned for"* (Isa. 6:7).

# DAY 23
# HEART CLEANSING FOR PURITY

*Create in me a pure heart, O God, and renew a steadfast spirit within me* (Ps. 51:10).

THIS WEEK'S quest has been a journey that calls for undivided loyalty to God and His will and plan for our lives. Such undivided loyalty becomes a component of purity. Yesterday, our quest pointed us to God's fire as a symbol of His purifying ability. It's important at this juncture that we not assume that undivided loyalty or even the blamelessness illustrated in Abraham's life can be ours by simply deciding that will be the direction of our lives. We need much more than focused willpower.

It's true that God offers us salvation. We do not earn or deserve it. Salvation is His gift. It's also true that God allows us to use our free will to decide to serve Him. Beyond that initial decision, we continue to exercise free will daily in deciding our level of openness to God's control in our lives. We need more than free will, resolve, and determination, however. Remember Peter's resolve discussed on Day 4. He and his friends resolved to walk with Jesus right into the jaws of death. That resolve folded quickly when opposition struck.

Peter and company needed something more; so do we. We need God's fire applied to our hearts just as Isaiah experienced it. Today's Bible study offers us a crystal-clear prayer for this very thing. Listen closely to David's prayer and apply his insights to your life. See what you can learn from David's example.

Ps. 51 finds David more than a year after his adultery with Bathsheba. He's in big trouble with God and himself, and he knows it. His prayer deals with two distinct spiritual needs: (1) God's forgiveness of past sins, and (2) his forgiven heart to be cleansed from the tendency to sin. We will focus primarily on the second need. Read Ps. 51:1-12 in preparation for today's study.

SIN

The first section of material considers our need for God's forgiveness. Notice David's call for God's mercy, unfailing love, great compassion, and ability to blot transgressions from the divine record. David testifies that his sins haunt him daily. Sin always haunts. David states an important spiritual truth when he says we not only hurt ourselves and innocent victims when we sin but also hurt God. That's the primary hurt. David has been caught red-handed in his sin, and he acknowledges that he deserves God's judgment for it.

ALWAYS

HAUNTS.

Ps. 51:5 calls attention to the reason our hearts need cleansing. The NIV translation of this verse obscures the original meaning, which is "Surely in iniquity I was born." In other words, we come into this world with a human nature turned inward on self. From infancy we prefer our own interests, even if they go against God's will for our lives. Our hearts need cleansing because they are tainted with the self-sovereignty problem passed down from our original parents.

In verse 6 David says, "Surely you desire truth in the inner parts; you teach me wisdom in the inmost place," as he highlights our need for God to deal with our "inner parts" or our "inmost place." We never solve the problem of sinning by coming up with a longer list of rules or putting more police officers on the streets. The problem is solved only at its source where the desire to sin begins.

In the first part of the prayer, David focused on his act of sin. In the second part, he focused on his human nature that urged him to sin. Then he pleaded for God's cleansing. The literal meaning of the word used here for "cleanse" is "un-sin me." David calls for more than an outward or ceremonial cleansing with a hyssop in the forgiveness of his sinful acts. He needs a divine washing of his inner nature. David's call for two cleansings implies that he seeks a work from God that will make his heart so pure that no figure of speech or no ceremony can capture it.

Beyond the washing, he seeks an inner transformation to change him from the inside out. Only then will he get back his joy, gladness, and rejoicing. He can rejoice again only after he knows that God no longer sees the sin.

The following verses are the focal point of today's Bible study: "Create in me a pure heart, O God, and renew a steadfast spirit within me. Do not cast me from your presence or take your Holy Spirit from me. Restore to me the joy of your salvation and grant me a willing spirit, to sustain me" (Ps. 51:10-12). Here lies the heart of the matter. God's forgiveness of our sins is essential, but forgiveness is never enough. David drilled to the source of sin in his human nature. He prays for God to deal decisively with that sinful nature. This prayer for purity asks God for three things: (1) a clean heart, (2) a right spirit, and (3) a sense of God's Spirit living within him.

The ministry of the Spirit in the hearts of all believers as we know it today did not come to full reality until the Day of Pentecost. And yet, David hits on something here that stands out in salvation history as an important spiritual insight. In some ways, David was ahead of his time in understanding what we all need in order to solve the sin problem. We need clean hearts. If God renewed David, and if the Spirit indwelt him as he requested, he knew he would get back the joy of his salvation and a willing spirit to persevere to the end.

Today's Bible study reminds us that people haven't changed much since David's time. David penned these words more than 3,000 years ago, yet the needs of the human heart have remained rather constant. People still come into this world with a desire to please themselves. They use free will to choose their own ways, and they wake up one day deeper in sin than they realized was possible. Yes, more than anything they need forgiveness for their acts of sinning. Once forgiven, they need God to cleanse their hearts of the desire to sin or serve self.

Thankfully, God knows us better than we know ourselves. That's why He planted the desire for purity deep within us. He wouldn't plant a desire He didn't intend to fulfill. David analyzed his need correctly. He named our need as well. God can help us; He provides two cleansings!

# Day 23

**Remember:**

Purity requires God to cleanse our hearts.

*Create in me a pure heart, O God, and renew a steadfast spirit within me* (Ps. 51:10).

# Day 24

# DECLARE YOURSELF DOA

*Count yourselves dead to sin but alive to God in Christ Jesus* (Rom. 6:11).

YESTERDAY we studied David's prayer for a clean heart. But let's be careful not to miss something important. It's easy for us to see why David needed God's forgiveness and help; he committed adultery with his neighbor and orchestrated a plan that resulted in her husband's untimely death. He broke up a home and murdered a man! You may be thinking, *Well, I've never done anything that bad.* That's probably true. But you're not off the hook!

We find ways to make excuses for ourselves! I remember a discussion in my university classroom when I asked students to define sin. Rather than defining it, they chose to illustrate it. They named premeditated murder and child abuse as sin. When I asked who among them could be classified as a sinner, none could, of course. None had performed murder or child abuse. They had set the bar so low that none of them qualified.

It is easy to "rate" sin. Premeditated murder rates much higher on the scale than cheating on income taxes. God does not use our scale. Sin breaks God's law, and it breaks God's heart. Everyone, including believers, must guard against rationalizing sin or explaining it away.

Believers sometimes subconsciously slip into this trap. Forgiveness of past sins and new birth as a new creature in Christ become the high-water mark of life. God works in us to give us singing hearts and testimonies of His matchless grace. Once we encounter a spiritual lack, as described on Day 4, however, we may have a tendency to hide it from ourselves or make excuses for our need. We haven't willfully turned our backs on God, so what gives? We feel frustrated.

In yesterday's Bible study, David asked God to do two things in his heart and life: forgive him of his sins and cleanse him from the thing that pushed him to sin in the first place. I especially like David's request at the end of Ps. 51:12, "Grant me a willing spirit." He needed something changed in his nature. He needed God to change his "want to."

What is that nature change David needed? How does the need manifest itself in believers' lives? In Rom. 6:11-14, Paul said it becomes the source of evil desires and tries to entice us to use our bodies as "instruments of wickedness" (v. 13). He warned Roman believers to not allow sin to master them.

What is Paul talking about? He is talking about living a life that insists on its own way, or even worse, Satan's way. This way of life puts self first and centers the universe around personal motivations. It manifests itself in self-will, self-love, self-trust, and self-exaltation. It seeks pleasure, power, position, and whatever else it wants. It places its own needs over those of others.

These characteristics show up among Christians and non-Christians alike, both in the business world and in the church. We can demonstrate these attitudes toward both God and other people. While not an exhaustive list, the following makes the point!

- Self-centered: Acting as if the earth and all other planets in this universe revolve around your head.
- Self-assertive: Moving to the front of the line because you deserve to be first; having to win every table game.
- Self-deprecating: Calling undue attention to yourself by putting yourself down in order to get others to praise you.

- Self-conceited: Acting as if you are God's gift to humanity.
- Self-advancing: Manipulating people and circumstances to favor or benefit yourself.
- Self-indulgent: Looking primarily after your own wants and needs.
- Self-pleasing: Making sure your family or group eats where you want to eat and watches the television program you want to watch—every time.
- Self-seeking: Being so in love with yourself that your primary responsibility in life is to assure your own happiness.
- Self-pity: Feeling sorry for yourself because you are so deprived, overweight, underweight, plagued, or whatever else darkens your world.
- Self-defense: Always making excuses to justify your behavior.
- Self-sufficiency: Living as if you need no one else's help, not even God's help.
- Self-consciousness: Being so concerned about how you look or the impression you make on others that you accomplish little else; always worrying about what other people think.
- Self-preoccupied: Being so narrowly focused on your own interests and needs that you are not aware of the world around you.
- Self-introspective: Keeping your finger on your psychological, emotional, or spiritual pulse at all times and monitoring every wavelength that passes through your brain.
- Self-righteous: Getting blessed at the incredible blessing and contribution you are to God's work and proud of your good example.
- Self-glorying: Calling attention to your ministry and spiritual accomplishments and amazing even yourself at just how good you are.

- Self-proclaiming: Announcing to everyone that you are God's answer to folks' prayers and declare your ways to be God's wishes in a particular situation.
- Self-made: Being proud of the fact that no one gave you money or supported you while you were getting to where you are today.

What is the result of this pattern? It damages and destroys relationships with family members, friends, and other Christian believers. It short-circuits concern for others. It creates dissension and tension. It ultimately results in loneliness and lack of fulfillment. It leaves a wake of evil and corruption. Satan told Eve in the garden, "You will not die." He lied.

No quest for purity is complete without dealing with the sin buried deep within human nature. It's buried so deep that some believers fail to recognize its presence for a long time. This sin principle almost always brings the spiritual hindrance discussed on Day 4. You must declare your self-centered nature DOA (dead on arrival) when you bring this problem to God and ask for His help. If you've encountered the problem but have not dealt decisively with it, you are a perfect candidate for Discovery 3. You can experience purity for the life you've longed for!

# DAY 24

## Remember:

You must declare your self-centered nature DOA when you come to God for His help.

*Count yourselves dead to sin but alive to God in Christ Jesus* (Rom. 6:11).

# UNDIVIDED LOYALTY

*Jesus answered, "If you want to be perfect, go, sell your possessions and give to the poor, and you will have treasure in heaven. Then come, follow me"* (Matt. 19:21).

SUE AND I first met Carlos when we took our university students to Panama City on a spring break work trip. In the years that followed he hosted us on three more work trips throughout Central America and the Caribbean. Carlos impressed upon me the meaning of undivided loyalty to Christ. Let me tell you a little about him.

Carlos studied to be a medical doctor. While in medical school, he served as a faithful layperson in his church. He took some theology classes along with his medical classes to give him a better understanding of his Christian faith. This provided him with both religious and professional training. When an area church found itself between pastors, Carlos agreed to fill the pulpit for a few months. God used this experience to call him to full-time ministry.

Carlos had the potential to earn one of the largest salaries in his country as a medical doctor. Yet he chose to live in a modest home and earn a modest salary as he fulfilled God's call on his life. His undivided loyalty to Christ affected his entire life. His infectious smile, his sense of humor, and his abundant love for Christ witnessed to the reality of a life satisfaction that comes only from a reckless abandon to God's will.

The verse at the top of the page comes from Jesus' encounter with a rich young man. You can read the account in Matt. 19:16-22. Mark (10:17-30) and Luke (18:18-30) also relate Jesus' encounter. So, we gather several insights about the rich young man from the three accounts. His unusual spirituality and material wealth earned him a high reputation at an early age. Unlike the Pharisees who asked Jesus questions in hopes of tricking Him, the young man approached Jesus with the pure intention of asking an honest question. His spiritual sensitivity led him to a religious puzzle that begged for a solution.

In Jesus' day it was taught that God granted eternal life based on the satisfactory performance of particular religious or benevolent acts. This way of thinking still receives a lot of attention. The average person on the street believes in eternal life coming through God's favorable judgment of our outward actions. There were various lists of essential religious and benevolent acts circulating during Jesus' day. These included practices such as praying, fasting, and giving to the needy. The young man in this story wanted to be sure he followed the right list to assure eternal life. He recognized Jesus' authority and wanted to get His final word on the subject.

Jesus pointed him to the Ten Commandments. His reference to the One who is good (God) covers the first four. His reference to commandments numbers 5, 6, 7, 8, and 9 can all be summed up with "love your neighbor as yourself." Jesus failed to mention commandment number 10, "Do not covet." I wonder why. Jesus' answer disappointed the young man, because he regarded it as too simple. He'd followed the commandments perfectly, or so he thought. Yet, he still had not secured peace of mind or certainty of his salvation.

Jesus gives the requirement for the young man to be perfect. He makes a specific prescription for reaching this standard. The young man must deal with his internal problem of coveting (Commandment 10) by outwardly letting go of the material possessions he loves most. These possessions defined him; people spoke of him in terms of his great wealth. So, he needed to let go of these possessions that blocked a clear path to God.

Bible scholars agree that Jesus' particular advice to this young man does not apply equally to all believers. In other words, Jesus does not condemn owning material possessions or working a job that pays a salary. He requires us to remove all stumbling blocks that stand between us and fellowship with God and His will for our lives.

Why did Jesus require this level of commitment? The answer lies in the last phrase of Jesus' command, "Come, follow me." That's the same command and call to reckless abandon of personal ambitions that Jesus gave all of His disciples. They cast everything aside to follow Jesus. His command remains the same today for us.

In order to be pure in heart, we must remove all stumbling blocks that stand between us and fellowship with God and His will for our lives. We must keep a light touch on our possessions, social status, desires, ambitions, and goals in life. We must adopt God's perspective for self-denial. Everything we have is at the disposal of God and His direction.

The young man in this story needed to let go of wealth, the trinkets it purchased, and the status it earned him with people in his community. Once the young man saw the price tag on discipleship with Jesus, he walked away from the deal.

Apparently the price tag was too high. What an amazing realization for a man who had the power to buy anything, regardless of the price tag. Jesus required something the young man couldn't afford. His tastes and comfort levels were too high for that. Ironic, isn't it? The very thing to which he clung tightly for security and satisfaction would cost him his eternal life.

We read this story and say to ourselves, "How sad." Before you judge the young man too quickly, ask, *Does this story offer me a warning as well?* You bet. We've talked previously about giving God everything and consecrating ourselves completely to Him. We've talked about living in the world but not of it. We've talked about living as a sacrifice to God. We've talked about complete devotion to His cause. All of these concepts sound admirable and deeply spiritual. We know the ideas, but can we make the application to our daily lives? I mean, can we find practical ways to put feet to our good intentions?

We must also watch for subtle stumbling blocks to our spiritual commitment. These include anything that means more to you than pleasing God completely. Such stumbling blocks will make you weak and ineffective in your commitment to Christ because they divide your commitment. Once you remove them, you clear the path to heart purity.

# DAY 25

## Remember:
Heart purity requires an undivided loyalty.

*Go, sell your possessions and give to the poor, and you will have treasure in heaven. Then come, follow me* (Matt. 19:21).

# HEART PURE

*Blessed are the pure in heart, for they will see God* (Matt. 5:8).

I HATE the bait and switch. You know what I mean. I see a product advertised in the newspaper at a great price. I take the advertisement circular with me to the store to show the sales clerk a picture of what I want. The sales clerk politely informs me that my item is currently out of stock. But he tells me they have a much better product that costs only $50 more. The store baited me with the advertisement then tried to switch me to a higher-priced product once they got me into the store.

The bait and switch sometimes occurs in our quest for purity. We read the Bible and talk with Christian friends about God's provision for our spiritual development and maturity. We know God's Word calls us to purity, so we pursue it. Then, somehow during the process we find we've been switched to performance-based approval. As long as we perform according to expectations, we consider ourselves pure. We do what we're supposed to do and avoid evil. We begin to think we're doing great and the work belongs to us, but then we begin to feel the strain of failure when we underperform. That can lead to a boatload of frustration and guilt.

Now, don't get me wrong. Becoming a Christian always leads naturally into a new lifestyle that flows from becoming a new creature in Christ. Hence, we quit doing that which displeases God and begin doing all that pleases Him. Your friends need not be licensed fruit inspectors to recognize the godly fruit produced in your new life.

It becomes problematic, however, if we attempt to reduce our Christian lifestyle into a codified checklist of duties. That can quickly suck the life right out of the lifestyle. Acceptable scores on the performance slowly replace vital relationship with Christ. We must constantly guard against slipping into performance-oriented purity.

WHEN YOUR HEART IS PURE, YOU SEE GOD.

Purity of heart is singleness of purpose for God's will and way. The person who possesses this singleness of purpose is the opposite of double-minded. James 1:8 says a double-minded man is "unstable in all he does." James 4:8 says, "Come near to God and he will come near to you. Wash your hands, you sinners, and purify your hearts, you double-minded."

"Double-minded" describes the person who vacillates in his or her choices between the mind of the flesh and the mind of the Spirit. Such a person wants to go God's way but also wants to go his or her own way, hesitating between God's preferences and his or her own. Do you want as much of God as you can grasp in one hand while holding on to as much of yourself as you can grasp with the other? That is divided loyalty.

James calls for single-mindedness for the purposes of God. He would define holiness as "to will one thing," that is, God's will. Jesus presented this same idea in today's Bible verse. A pure heart desires only to please God, without personal agendas or private plans for self-advancement. More than anything, the person with a pure heart wants to find and do God's will. Jesus promised that such a person will see God, both in the daily affairs of this life and in heaven for all eternity.

So does single-mindedness classify a believer as pure in heart? If you're talking perfect performance, the answer is no. Maturity and growth bring that. If you're talking about perfect motive or desire to please God, the answer is yes. More than anything in the world, a complete openness to God increases your desire to please Him.

One day during our first full summer of living in Kansas, I was adding a room and deck to our house, and the heat was stifling. Brent played with his toy trucks in a dirt pile near my construction site. He disappeared into the house for a few minutes then emerged through the kitchen door with a glass of ice water for me. He held it in my direction and said, "Here you go, Dad." I could tell he was proud of himself for thinking of me. That big smile on his face warmed my heart in places the sun could never reach. I took the glass and drank it right down. I thanked him for his thoughtfulness. We talked for a minute, and he went back to playing in the dirt, contented that he had demonstrated his love for his dad.

I learned a lesson that day about the difference between intention and performance. You see, Brent failed to wash the dirt from his hands before he grabbed a handful of ice cubes for my glass of water. He got about as much dirt in my glass as he had on his hands. As his dad, I saw right past his imperfect performance to his pure act of love.

Was Brent's performance perfect? You tell me. It was as far as I could tell! And you can rest assured your Heavenly Father feels the same way about your efforts on your quest for purity. Is your action always flawless? No. Can the desire of your heart be pure and clean? You bet.

Offer yourself completely to the Father. Let Him purify your heart by faith. Let Him have your performance score cards as well. Let Him catch the guilt balls that come your way following a flawed performance. As we've said so many times before on this quest, the key to experiencing purity for the life you've longed for comes from a close walk with God. When your heart is pure, you see God—both now and later.

# Day 26

**Remember:**

You can be heart pure with a single-minded heart toward God.

*Blessed are the pure in heart, for they will see God* (Matt. 5:8).

# DISCOVERY 4
## YOU CAN RECEIVE POWER.

## Memory Verse for the Week

*But you will receive power when the Holy Spirit comes
on you; and you will be my witnesses in Jerusalem,
and in all Judea and Samaria, and to the ends of the earth*
(Acts 1:8).

# DAY 27
# WHERE DO I LOOK?

*When Simon saw that the Spirit was given at the laying on of the apostles' hands, he offered them money and said, "Give me also this ability so that everyone on whom I lay my hands may receive the Holy Spirit"* (Acts 8:18-19).

JERRY called me one Saturday morning to ask a favor. He wanted to surprise Angela, his teenager, with a brand-new, bright red sports car. He asked me to drive it from the car dealership to his home. I was excited beyond description. I had never driven this car model before. On the way to the dealership I pictured me in that red sports car peeling out of the parking lot with a cloud of smoke trailing! I could surely go 0 to 60 in less than 7 seconds!

I was snapped back to reality as we pulled into the dealership. The bright red sports car sat proudly in front of the showroom floor. Jerry signed a few papers and dropped the keys to roadway conquest in my hands. I could hardly wait to get this finely tuned machine on the freeway. As I reached the freeway, I punched the accelerator. Guess what? Nothing happened. I don't mean my acceleration seemed a little sluggish; I mean, nothing happened! I think some factory worker mistakenly placed a lawn mower motor under the hood of this beautiful red sports car.

I couldn't wait to tell Jerry about the new car's engine problem when we reached his driveway. He said, "Yes, I know. I didn't want my daughter to be tempted with too much power, so I ordered the smallest engine the factory makes." What a paradox! A bright red sports car that screamed speed powered by an engine that could hardly move it? Something's wrong with that picture.

I think many believers suffer from the same power-shortage disappointment. We know we need power to live the Christian life. God places an unmistakable quest for power within us. No minister or Christian friend has to tell us we need power; we intuitively know we need it. Yet, our daily performance does not always match our expectations for this power. So, the quest continues.

We turn to God's Word for an understanding of God's power. We read about His power throughout the Bible. It tells of His creation power (Ps. 65:6) and His power over nature (Luke 8:25). It speaks of His mighty deeds and awesome acts, especially related to delivering His people from Egypt (Num. 14:13). The Bible recounts the story of the Exodus in great detail throughout the Bible. There is no doubt of God's infinite power. As Job put it, "I know that you can do all things; no plan of yours can be thwarted" (42:2). The Bible tells us that God's greatest demonstration of power occurred when He raised Jesus from death (Rom. 1:4). We're not likely to doubt God's ability to perform mighty acts in nature and in human life.

What's more, the Bible indicates that God demonstrates His power through believers. In today's Scripture lesson, Philip preached the gospel in Samaria. God confirmed Philip's message with miraculous signs that amazed the citizens. Simon, a man from Samaria, also amazed the townfolk with miraculous signs. Simon convinced people that he represented God with his great powers. Philip's signs were different from Simon's because they came from the hand of God; Simon used slight-of-hand magic to amaze people.

Peter and John soon arrived in Samaria to continue the spiritual revival started under Philip's ministry. Everyone realized Peter, John, and Philip demonstrated God's power unlike anything they had seen before, even from the hands of Simon. They were especially impressed with the change in believers' lives after receiving the Spirit.

Simon also knew these Christians had something he needed. But he made a big mistake. He tried to purchase a local franchise for God's power. He saw it as a commodity to be secured or possessed rather than an experience and a relationship with God. Peter's negative reaction in Acts 8:20-23 indicates the severity of Simon's mistake. God's power displayed in believers is not a commodity, and it cannot be purchased. Peter says the condition of a believer's heart and deliverance from sin set the stage for the relationship with God that is necessary to display God's power.

Believers today often have a power-shortage disappointment when comparing their lives to demonstrations of God's power they read about in the Bible. They may expect to go from 0 to 60 in 7 seconds, so to speak, but realize they don't quite have what it takes for such peek performance. Something's missing. They cannot speak like Peter or perform miracles like Philip.

What should they do? They may decide that God only offers His power to special people or to ordinary people for special occasions. This is just not their time, they reason. Or, they may decide, like Simon, that God has a secret formula for unlocking His power in their lives; they must discover or purchase this formula.

Such conclusions lead believers away from the Christian path and onto dangerous detours in search of magical divine power for spiritual life. None of these detours ever satisfy the power-shortage disappointment. So, please don't be lured by false advertising that offers you spiritual power through gimmicks, purchases, or mail-in offers.

When I traveled away from home during Brent's childhood, I always brought him a small gift from wherever I visited. He proudly displayed my gifts on shelves in his bedroom. It always warmed my heart when I reunited with my family following a trip away from home. As soon as Sue, Brent, and I hugged, my son would ask, "What did you bring me, Daddy?" For a while I wondered if it was my safe return or my gift he appreciated more. Looking back, I can see he valued me more.

If we're not careful, we can inadvertently focus our quest so completely on the search for spiritual power that we find ourselves wanting to see or perform miraculous signs and wonders more than we want a close relationship with God. May that never happen to you! Guard carefully against a perverted redirection of your quest.

This week as you seek the power for the life you've longed for, don't seek it as the prize to be grasped. Rather, let it happen as a natural result of your relationship with the Spirit of Christ. We're going to pursue this quest for power from several different directions, always centered around our relationship with the Spirit of Christ. Seek the giver of the gift, not just the gift.

Maybe it's really not a "where" question at all. Maybe the question is "To whom do I look for spiritual power?" Focus your attention on that thought today as you keep your priorities in perspective.

# Day 27

## Remember:
The question is not *Where do I look?* but *To whom do I look?* when seeking God's power.

*When Simon saw that the Spirit was given at the laying on of the apostles' hands, he offered them money* (Acts 8:18).

# IT'S IN THE BANK

*I pray that out of his glorious riches he may strengthen you with power through his Spirit in your inner being, so that Christ may dwell in your hearts through faith. And I pray that you, being rooted and established in love, may have power, together with all the saints, to grasp how wide and long and high and deep is the love of Christ, and to know this love that surpasses knowledge—that you may be filled to the measure of all the fullness of God (Eph. 3:16-19).*

RECENTLY, one of my students requested prayer for her brother. She told our class about his unusual situation. She and her brother grew up in an expensive home in an extremely wealthy neighborhood. Once her brother reached adulthood, he rejected his parents' values and lifestyle. He protested their affluence to the point that he moved out of the family home even though he had nowhere to go. At the time of my student's prayer request for her brother's health and safety, he was sleeping on city streets and eating from garbage cans.

The young man's father provided for his son in case he changed his mind by placing a large sum of money in a bank on the street where his son slept. He gave his son a checkbook for the account with the instructions, "If you ever need money, all you have to do is walk into the bank and write a check."

It doesn't get any easier than that, does it? No reason for the son to ever be cold or go hungry. Most people would consider the son fortunate to have such a generous father. What's more, most would consider the money readily accessible. The father did everything he knew to provide for his son. All that was required of the boy was to walk into the bank and ask for his money.

Our Bible text for today talks about a power from God that we long for. From what Paul says, it sounds like God has done for us something like what this father did for his son. God prompts a longing in our hearts to find power for our lives and then provides a way for us to access that power.

The power you long for comes directly from God. He provides it to us from His glorious riches. Paul has the image of an inexhaustible resource that overflows on our behalf. This power comes through the indwelling presence of the Spirit of Christ. He doesn't just visit us on special occasions or when difficult circumstances come our way; He lives with us every moment of every day.

We see the close cooperative efforts of Christ and the Spirit working in us. That's why I refer to Him as the Spirit of Christ. We cannot discern the difference between the two who work within us. When Paul speaks of our inner being, he's thinking about that part of us from which emerges our personality and our spirituality. It's the place where God lets us know He has pardoned our sins and accepted us into His family. It's the seat of our praise, worship, and gratitude for Him. It's the source of our willpower. It's the fountain from which our emotions spring. It's the root of our attitudes. It's the location of our conscience. It's the place we draw up plans for our actions and reactions in life. The source of all these is in our inner being. That's why it is so important for the Spirit of Christ to dwell there continually and completely. He must flavor everything that springs from our inner being.

How do we get this power for the life we long for? Paul says it comes by our faith in God. We trust His promise to provide for our need and depend on Him daily for His supply. The rooting and establishing of this power is found in God's love. Rooting speaks of a tree's foundation; establishing speaks of a building's foundation. Both trees and buildings must have solid foundations to survive the winds of time. Only God's love working within us gives us the solid foundation we need to complete our spiritual journey with victory. The love Paul speaks of here refers to several loves: the love of the Father, Son, and Spirit for one another, the love of the triune God for us, our love for God, and our love for other people.

This power is not just for a select few; it is for all of God's saints—including you. When Paul uses the measurement concepts of wide, long, high, and deep, it sounds like he is describing a building. It's not a brick or wooden building, however. It's a spiritual building of sorts. Both you as an individual and your entire community of faith make this building. God and His love dwell completely in you, and you are able to understand Christ's love, a love that surpasses all human knowledge. God gives you an understanding in your heart that you feel and know but cannot adequately put into words. It moves you through life with a power that defies description. Even Paul's thoughts in this passage defy description!

Paul uses many lofty concepts in today's Scripture. He saves the greatest for last. He says this power fills us with God himself. Imagine that. We may never be recognized by the world as having celebrity status or political importance. We may never win an award or have a building named after us. We may live our entire lives without notice from the media. All the while, we can have the greatest power in the universe dwelling within our hearts—the presence of Creator God himself!

We are reminded by this lesson that God makes power available for His children. This power does not come from discovering a code to secret knowledge or a ritual to certain religious practices. If a code or a ritual could access it, it would soon fall into the hands of those who would misuse it for their own purposes. Remember Simon from yesterday's study? He wanted God's power so he could impress his fellow citizens. God's power is not for sale and not to be used for personal gain. We must always guard our motives and ask God's Spirit to help us see our hearts as He sees them. We must never want power for wrong or selfish reasons.

God's power comes your way through relationship with the Spirit of Christ. His Spirit does not simply visit you occasionally or offer you special abilities. He worked that way with people in the Old Testament. However, since Pentecost, He dwells constantly within those who seek Him. Receiving God's power requires no special formula. You need only ask Him in faith for it.

Read the Scripture passage again. Notice that while power is referred to several times, power is never the subject of the quest. The Spirit of Christ is the focus of your quest. Seek Him, not power, just as children should love traveling parents more than the gifts they bring when they return. God's power comes as a by-product of your relationship with Him. As a result of your relationship with the Spirit of Christ, Paul says you will receive, along with God's power, the love of Christ and the fullness of God.

---

# DAY 28

## Remember:
God has provided all you need for victorious Christian living.

*I pray that out of his glorious riches he may strengthen you with power through his Spirit in your inner being* (Eph. 3:16).

# POWER OVER SIN

*But if we walk in the light, as he is in the light, we have fellowship with one another, and the blood of Jesus, his Son, purifies us from all sin. . . . My dear children, I write this to you so that you will not sin* (1 John 1:7; 2:1).

FOR THE PAST two days, we've looked at spiritual power in a rather general sense. It's time to get more specific. We must ask ourselves a very important question as we seek power for the life we've longed for. That question is simply, *Power for what?* For the next several days we will explore that question from several different perspectives. Each perspective will offer more specific insights into the power God makes available for His children.

We have established that God does not offer us power to perform miraculous signs and wonders so that we can amaze people. Simon sought this type of power in Acts 8 and received correction from Peter. God does not offer us power so we can be like Superman or Wonder Woman. Such powers make great cartoons and novels, but they serve little purpose in the lives of Christian believers. We have also concluded that God does not offer power to feed our personal egos. We must guard against wanting God to work through us in a manner that would somehow result in personal gain.

God offers us power, first of all, to live above habitual sinning. John makes the point clearly in our text for today, "If we walk in the light, as he is in the light . . . the blood of Jesus, his

Son, purifies us from all sin" and "so that you will not sin" (1 John 1:7; 2:1).

God forgives us of past sins, but is forgiveness all God can offer us? Are we on our own from that point forward? What can we do to help ourselves so we don't return to old habits? Not much. We can exercise large quantities of willpower or turn over a tree-full of new leaves. But, that's about it. Only the power of God can radically change us at the core of our beings to break old habits of sinning.

It's a crucial question: "Once I've sinned, am I hopelessly programmed to repeat my mistakes as long as I live?" In other words, are we all doomed to sin throughout our lives? Is our battle against sin hopeless? Absolutely not—to all of these questions!

There is good news. Not only can God forgive us of our past sins, but He also has the power to change us from within and reorient our nature so we can return to His will and plan for our lives. He can restore us to His original purpose for us in the garden. No, we don't have physical walks with God every day, but we do fellowship continually with Him through His Spirit. God's power can forgive us for breaking His law and His heart. Furthermore, God's power can change us from within, at a heart level, to break the cycle of sinning. This is how we can live according to the original garden plan. Now we can be what God wants us to be—not by ourselves, but by the power of His Spirit living within us. Yes, God has power for us to live above habitual sinning!

Here are other crucial questions: *Will I always prefer my ways over God's ways? Will I always use my freewill to choose my own way? Is self-preference a permanent feature of who I am?* Again, absolutely not! Along with the power to live above habitual sinning, God also offers us power to live beyond self-preference, and His power can cleanse us from self-preference.

Some Christians believe sin's habitual power and our self-preference is a curse we will live with our whole lives. They think we're doomed to repeat our past sins, though we may hate to do it. They see this as a hopeless cycle beyond repair during our lifetimes. These Christians have not discovered God's power over sin, both as an act and as a principle of human nature. They're living below their means like the young man I described yesterday who lived on the streets with money in the bank.

Let's quickly review God's provision for us. His plan of salvation—to restore us to the original intention He had for us—begins with faith in Jesus Christ. By trusting in Christ's death on Calvary and resurrection from the dead, the Father forgives us of our past sins and adopts us into His family. As we walk in daily fellowship with Him, we are no longer deprived of His presence, which Adam and Eve lost in the garden. Forgiveness is wonderful, but it is not enough. We must have God's power to break sin's stranglehold and reorient us from within so we can continue to live every day as His children.

Sin creates a twofold problem. God's forgiveness takes care of my past sins. That long list constitutes Problem 1. But what about sin's nature buried deep within me that causes me to want to do the wrong thing or "my thing" in the first place? What about that pride that boasts to the world, "I did it my way"? That's Problem 2.

Self-preference lurks at the heart of this matter. It remains deeply rooted in my being even after God forgives my sins. I enjoy God's forgiveness and fellowship, but part of me wants to retain at least some sense of control.

This attitude, or mind-set, highlights the second problem that needs God's touch. It's not that I want to purposefully sin against Him. I'm not hoping to harbor some sinful habit or spirit. It's just that I want to retain some autonomy about the direction of my life. Why should someone else get to call all the shots? Why should I surrender control of everything?

Take a deeper look at this. When you give your heart and

life to Christ in conversion, you give Him everything of your-self that you know to give Him at the time.

Then, you begin to live as a Christian in your actions, thoughts, attitudes, motives, reactions, possessions, habits, and all the rest. Unfortunately, you may move a few personal items to one very small room in your life. Not anything big and bad, just something to represent autonomy.

God eventually zeros in on autonomy. It's impossible to be-long totally to God and keep anything from Him. When I rec-ognize any attitude or mind-set as a hindrance in my spiritual progress and come to terms with the need to resolve it, I place myself in an excellent position for God's power to help me.

Again, the solution to Problem 2 is to surrender command of the control center of your life. Let God have complete con-trol of your past, present, and future—everything you are and everything you may ever become. Surrender all your hopes, dreams, goals, and aspirations to His leadership. That's the se-cret to God's power over self-preference.

Yes, God can give you power over sin to live the life you've longed for!

# DAY 29

## Remember:
God offers power to give us victory over sinful habits and self-preference.

*But if we walk in the light, as he is in the light, we have fellowship with one another, and the blood of Jesus, his Son, purifies us from all sin. . . . My dear children, I write this to you so that you will not sin* (1 John 1:7; 2:1).

# POWER OVER TRIALS AND TEMPTATIONS

*Consider it pure joy, my brothers, whenever you face trials of many kinds, because you know that the testing of your faith develops perseverance. Perseverance must finish its work so that you may be mature and complete, not lacking anything. . . . Blessed is the man who perseveres under trial, because when he has stood the test, he will receive the crown of life that God has promised to those who love him. When tempted, no one should say, "God is tempting me." For God cannot be tempted by evil, nor does he tempt anyone; but each one is tempted when, by his own evil desire, he is dragged away and enticed. Then, after desire has conceived, it gives birth to sin; and sin, when it is full-grown, gives birth to death* (James 1:2-4, 12-15).

OUR FAMILY plays a board game called The Magnificent Race. The game box describes it as a mad dash around the world. As with all board games, players must overcome a series of obstacles while progressing in the worldwide race. The arch villain of this board game is Dastardly Dan. Dan does everything in his power to discourage and bankrupt players. Victory comes only after numerous battles with this villain.

Christian living mirrors this board game in many ways. Believers make a magnificent journey through this life on earth. Most days seem like a mad dash against a nearly impossible schedule. Life would be so much easier without all of those appointments, carpools for the children, and meetings. Add family life at home, schoolwork, and church activities, and you have an action-packed day. In a perfect world all of the activities and responsibilities would dovetail together beautifully. In our less-than-perfect world they create tension and stress.

If these activities and responsibilities were our only problems, life might feel more manageable. They aren't. We must each deal with our own Dastardly Dan arch villain in the form of Satan. He's pinned a bull's-eye on our backs and targeted us for spiritual defeat. Our quest today takes us on a search for power to live victoriously over trials and temptations. The two concepts differ greatly. Temptations attempt to derail our faith; trials test and strengthen it.

In today's text, James instructs us regarding trials. James urges us to look on the positive side of our trials. It's usually hard for us to regard trials with "pure joy," but that's what James asks us to do. James calls attention to that which tries us rather than the process of the trial itself. In other words, he's thinking about the event, the experience, or the person(s) giving us difficulty. Rather than looking on these circumstances or people negatively, we should see them in terms of the good they produce in us. That's seldom easy to do.

What good results from trials? James lists four positive conclusions in verses 4-7.

1. We grow in patience (v. 4). We learn to outwait our circumstances. We develop spiritual muscles to persevere through situations that appear to be not in our favor. Paul echoes James's thought in Rom. 5:3, "We also rejoice in our sufferings, because we know that suffering produces perseverance."

2. We become mature and complete in our faith (vv. 4-5). The image reflects a grown person rather than a child. James envisions a veteran of the faith, not a young recruit. He sees a warrior who has stood tall in the heat of battle. He sees someone who has experienced a wide variety of experiences, both good and bad, across many years. This warrior has stayed true to the charge. He or she has weathered every battle to the point of being regarded as a mature soldier. That's what James sees happening to saints who grow through their trials.

3. We increase in faith (v. 6). We ask God for help and trust Him to answer our prayers. Through the entire process, we hold steady and remain confident that God will see us through. In so doing, our faith grows just as muscles increase through strenuous exercise. The opposite image of increased faith is the sea wave that rises and falls hourly as weather patterns change. All the benefits added to our spiritual lives come as gifts from God. We do not earn or deserve them. James refers to Him as "the giving God." His very nature is that of a giver. We must never take His gifts for granted.

4. We receive a reward from God (v. 7). When we ask for God's help in faith and persevere, we can count on Him to give us His help. It's important to emphasize that the reward spoken of here is not an object we seek. It's not a thing God gives us. The reward is the spiritual life we enjoy through communion with Him. It's the fellowship shared between God and His children. When we look back later on the events or circumstances of our trials, we won't remember the facts of the event or circumstance nearly as clearly as we will remember the sweet presence of the Lord who held our hand or carried us through the entire experience. Viewed from that perspective, we can envision the pure joy James urges us to have.

James tells us, "Blessed is the man who perseveres under trial, because when he has stood the test, he will receive the crown of life that God has promised to those who love him" (1:12). In Matt. 5:3-11, Jesus also refers to events and experiences that appear negative on the surface. However, when viewed from the broader perspective of the benefits received, the person is actually blessed. Why? Because spiritual muscles grow, spiritual strength increases, and spiritual faith matures to make the person a seasoned warrior.

We tend to not think about the rewards that await us at the end. However, James mentions them here as an encouragement to press on. The word James uses pictures a wreath being placed around the neck of the first-place runner of a race. It's given at the victory celebration held at the conclusion of the race of faith. The crown of life refers not so much to a physical object as to the eternal life we have in the presence of our Lord. Our most cherished reward is uninterrupted fellowship with Him forever. That's the best blessing of all.

James warns us against surrendering to temptation in verses 13-15. Remember, temptation targets us for defeat. Paul gives us helpful instruction in 1 Cor. 10:12-14: "So, if you think you are standing firm, be careful that you don't fall! No temptation has seized you except what is common to man. And God is faithful; he will not let you be tempted beyond what you can bear. But when you are tempted, he will also provide a way out so that you can stand up under it. Therefore, my dear friends, flee from idolatry." Read his thoughts as you think about the nature and limits of temptation.

1. Temptation is a fact. We can engage in all manner of discussions about the nature of temptation in believers. However, this does not take us one step further away from temptation's reach. This passage reminds us of the stark truth: we will face temptation.

2. Temptation usually catches us off guard. Notice the warn-

ing of verse 12, which says, "So, if you think you are standing firm, be careful that you don't fall!" It's at the time you
feel confident of your solid standing that you may be most
vulnerable to falling. Never underrate the appeal of temptation. The best preparation for temptation's attack requires us to not overvalue our current position. Remember
what happened to Samson as he slept: "Then she called,
'Samson, the Philistines are upon you!'" (Judg. 16:20).

3. Temptation originates outside of us. Consider its source.
   There is a difference between a desire that comes from
   within you and one that comes at you from the world.
   Your heart may be as pure as the new-fallen snow and
   temptation will suggest to you behaviors that would not
   please God. So, examine your heart and keep it clean.

4. Temptation is universal. "Common to man" means
   every person on earth is tempted just like you are. Temptation crosses all language and cultural barriers. It makes
   no discrimination between age, race, gender, or social
   standing. It is a worldwide common denominator. Even
   Christ heard temptation's call.

5. Temptation has its limits. Satan would like for you to believe that temptation leaves you with no alternative but
   to yield. He wants you to think that sin is inevitable. But
   Satan is not all-powerful, and neither is temptation.
   Both can go just so far and no farther. God always sees
   to it that temptation's offer does not extend beyond His
   ability to empower you to resist it.

6. You can resist temptation. This is a simple, yet powerful
   truth. If Christian believers really grasp this truth, it will
   empower them to hold out for God's victory. Both Satan
   and temptation are finite, so both can be defeated. Sin is
   not inevitable. God promises to always provide a way
   out. When tempted, pray for God's resisting power, then
   look for His escape.

7. Once temptation passes, you'll be left standing. Verse 13 ends with a promise: "But when you are tempted, he will also provide a way out so that you can stand up under it." When the dust settles after your battle with temptation, you'll still be standing. Can you see yourself standing your ground as Satan flees in defeat? Christ offers us a good example in Matt. 4:1-11. He met Satan's temptations in one concentrated effort and at various times throughout His earthly ministry. Verse 11 tells us that after He resisted, "Then the devil left him, and the angels came and attended him." He remained victorious with every encounter. So can you!

# DAY 30

## Remember:

God gives us power to live victoriously over trials and temptations.

*Consider it pure joy, my brothers, whenever you face trials of many kinds, because you know that the testing of your faith develops perseverance* (James 1:2-3).

# POWER FOR WITNESS

*But in your hearts set apart Christ as Lord. Always be prepared to give an answer to everyone who asks you to give the reason for the hope that you have. But do this with gentleness and respect, keeping a clear conscience, so that those who speak maliciously against your good behavior in Christ may be ashamed of their slander* (1 Pet. 3:15-16).

THE QUICKEST WAY to throw both new and seasoned Christians into a full-blown power shortage is to tell them they must hit the streets as a witness for Christ. They quickly conjure up frightening images of embarrassing or stressful situations! By the time their imaginations get a full grasp of the possibilities, the prospect of sharing a word for Christ seems impossible.

Power to witness for Christ should not scare us. In 1 Pet. 3:15-16, Peter tells us to set Christ apart as Lord in our hearts. The original language says for us to "sanctify the Christ as Lord." He takes this phrase from Isa. 8:13: "The LORD Almighty is the one you are to regard as holy, he is the one you are to dread." This verse is blasphemy if Jesus Christ is not God. Peter urges us to regard Christ as holy and serve Him in reverence and awe. Just as Jesus taught us in the Lord's Prayer, found in Matt. 6:9-13, we must reverence or hallow God's name. This attitude toward God should flow from our inner being.

Once Christ is given the proper place in our hearts, we can

then prepare a personal testimony to share with others about our faith. Peter's direction here does not demand that we memorize a theological defense of the Christian religion. Rather, he's encouraging us to be ready to share our own salvation story in our own words. Think through your response to such questions as,

- How did you come to know the Lord as your personal Savior?
- In your own words, who is Jesus Christ?
- Why are you a Christian?
- What does faith in Jesus mean to you?
- How do you cope when the troubles of life close in on you?
- Why do you have such a positive outlook on life?
- Where is your hope?

We think through our personal statement, because we always want to be ready to give a reasoned response for our Christian hope, as Peter calls it. We speak up for two important reasons: (1) we want to defend God's truth, and (2) we want to assist the understanding, and hopefully salvation, of those who listen. Our presentation can be simple and must be personal.

In the last part of verse 15, Peter tells us, "But do this with gentleness and respect." Nothing could be worse than for a Christian to speak for Christ with a spirit of arrogance or superiority. A tone of judgment or condemnation should never be part of our conversations. It is important to approach the subject in a way that shows our weakness and dependence upon God's Spirit for the correct words to speak. Few Christians feel adequate for the task. That's good; a sense of inadequacy helps us depend more on God's strength and wisdom than our own.

Peter goes on to remind us of the importance of keeping a clear conscience. Paul also speaks about the importance of a clear conscience in 1 Tim. 1:5 and 1 Cor. 4:4 stressing the importance of our lives matching up with what we say about our faith in God. A person can memorize a powerful salvation story and tell it with conviction to all who will listen. But if the testimony of that person's lifestyle does not match what is being said, it hurts the cause of Christ more than it helps.

Your good conduct should be transparent for all to see. In this way, those who might speak against you will be ashamed of their untruthful words. Even if someone chooses to say such things about you, no one will listen to them or believe them. They will see for themselves that your life speaks otherwise.

Read John 9:25. It illustrates a personal testimony and offers us an example to follow. Jesus healed the man in the early part of chapter 9. The Pharisees gathered to investigate the incident. They believed Jesus violated their laws when He healed this man. The man's parents refused to involve themselves in the inquiry, because they feared they would lose worship privileges at the Temple. They insisted that the man speak for himself. After he had been asked a number of leading questions on two separate occasions, he gave this powerful testimony: "One thing I do know. I was blind but now I see!"

The man refused to engage in theological arguments. He knew as well as you know such arguments are fruitless. He refused to side with the Pharisees. He refused to remain silent. He did what you and I can do—he told his personal experience in his own words. His testimony was not dramatic and gave very little detail. But, it told about being touched by Jesus! The witness cut through the intellectual gymnastics of the Pharisees with his simple statement, "I was blind but now I see!"

The idea of sharing your testimony may conjure up frightening images of embarrassing or stressful situations. It doesn't have to be that way, you know. The story of Christ's work in our lives can flow from your lips as naturally as telling your neighbor about a great bargain at the shopping center. You don't have to be effervescent and dramatic. You just have to be real. People care more about your being genuine than they do about hearing a grandiose tale.

Sharing your personal stories about Jesus and your hope in Him are important elements in living Christian lives. Our quest for power includes a search for the strength and ability to witness for Christ. He's never been ashamed of you; you must never be ashamed of Him.

---

# DAY 31

**Remember:**

God has power to help us witness for Him.

*Always be prepared to give an answer to everyone who asks you to give the reason for the hope that you have* (1 Pet. 3:15).

# POWER FOR MAKING DISCIPLES

*Then Jesus came to them and said, "All authority in heaven and on earth has been given to me. Therefore go and make disciples of all nations, baptizing them in the name of the Father and of the Son and of the Holy Spirit, and teaching them to obey everything I have commanded you. And surely I am with you always, to the very end of the age"* (Matt. 28:18-20).

GOD'S KINGDOM on earth expands as new converts are discipled into the faith. It's happened daily since Jesus walked here. The path of Christian discipleship is not a solitary one. The members of a Christian community walk the path together, aiding and supporting one another along the way. Sometimes encouraging; sometimes lifting the load; sometimes carrying one another. Christian discipleship is not a "Jesus and me" venture. It requires the regular contribution of every member of Christ's Body on this earth.

Today's Bible study passage reminds us that each of us has a part to play in bringing the unsaved into Christ's fold. God invites us to join Him in His ministry of adding new converts to the Christian community. It's not within the natural ability of most of us to do this. As you read yesterday, we can quickly calculate a power shortage when we attempt to disciple new converts into God's kingdom by our own strength and ability. We can participate in this important ministry only as God empowers us.

The event described in Matt. 28:16-20 occurred at the end of Jesus' post-Resurrection ministry. The context of the passage seems to indicate that the 11 apostles of Jesus, along with other followers, heard Him deliver this challenge.

An interesting aside to this story reminds us that even Christ himself, with loving disciples bowing at His feet in worship, had followers who stood around the edges of the scene and doubted. Remember this: You cannot neglect the ministry God calls you to do for Him just because some people stand around the edges, criticizing your efforts. Doubters and critics surface just about everywhere. So, minister on—even in the shadow of your critics!

In this closing account in Matthew's Gospel, Jesus does at least three things. He declares His ultimate authority in verse 18 when He says, "All authority in heaven and on earth has been given to me." He commissions His apostles and us to spread the gospel message and make disciples in verses 19 through 20a: "Therefore go and make disciples of all nations, baptizing them in the name of the Father and of the Son and of the Holy Spirit, and teaching them to obey everything I have commanded you." And in verse 20b He promises to be with us every day of our lives: "And surely I am with you always, to the very end of the age."

Verse 18 also offers us a brief glimpse into a heavenly transaction. In ways we will never understand this side of eternity, Jesus' coming to earth, His death, and His resurrection increased His authority in all of creation. The Son of God received this authority from the Father. A new contract between God and humanity took effect. God opened a new way to salvation in this transaction. We now have daily relationship with God due to Christ's authority.

In verse 19 Jesus shares some of His authority with His disciples. This includes not only the disciples who were present with Jesus that day but also all disciples of Jesus who follow after, including you and me. In essence, Jesus deputizes us to participate with Him in getting the word out about this new contract with God. Here, then, we receive our commission to join Jesus in disciple-making.

Believers have different gifts and abilities. God has a place for each one of us in His kingdom work. Paul speaks of various roles we serve in the Christian community, including apostles, prophets, evangelists, pastors, and teachers (Eph. 4:11). He lists many other roles in 1 Cor. 12:7-11 and Rom. 12:6-8. These varying roles differ among us based on our different gifts, talents, abilities, and personalities. God uses each person in his or her own unique way to contribute to the growth and development of His kingdom. That's why Paul takes extra effort to explain the importance of recognizing and coordinating various strengths and weaknesses in 1 Cor. 12:12-31.

In the Scripture passage for today, however, Jesus gives a commission to all of us. He does not reserve disciple-making only for preachers or evangelists. He challenges us all. We are to:

- Go
- Make disciples in all nations
- Baptize them into faith and
- Teach them the doctrines and lifestyle for Christ's followers.

In the last part of verse 20, Jesus promises to be with us. Matthew began and ended his book with this reminder. He began in 1:23 by calling Mary's child "Immanuel," which means "God with us." In 28:20, Jesus extends His presence to us even after He returns to heaven. He promises to remain with us for as long as we live. He fulfilled that promise by sending His Spirit (John 14:18 and Acts 2:1-4). That is why we call Him the Spirit of Christ in this book.

Jesus charges every word in this passage with an urgent

challenge. He balances His great challenge to go into all the world and make disciples with a great promise to boost our courage. We don't go out to the nations alone. We don't devise our own plans. We don't create our own strategies. With the aid of His Spirit, we face the challenge to make disciples by receiving the direction and strength from Christ himself! Partnering together with the Creator of the universe to make disciples for His kingdom—now that's power!

He promises to be with us, not just on our difficult days or our heavy ministry days, but every day! You expect God to draw near to you when you're being tempted, tried, persecuted, or challenged as a result of your faith. But, Jesus says He will be with you on your great days and even your ordinary, run-of-the-mill days. Now that's a Friend who sticks by your side closer than a brother or sister. He'll be with you right until you cross over to the other side; then, He'll welcome you across the threshold of heaven's door.

# Day 32

**Remember:**
God has the power to help us make disciples for Him.

*Go and make disciples of all nations* (Matt. 28:19).

# RECEIVING THE POWER

*But you will receive power when the Holy Spirit comes on you; and you will be my witnesses in Jerusalem, and in all Judea and Samaria, and to the ends of the earth* (Acts 1:8).

OUR QUEST this week has taken us on a search for power for the life we long for. We've talked about a variety of concepts that both describe and fail to describe this divine power. Ten days elapsed between the time Jesus promised His disciples that they would receive this power and the time they actually received it. They had no idea what form this power would take. They knew only that they would need a great deal of His help if they hoped to be successful in all He called them to do to advance His kingdom on earth.

You, like Jesus' disciples, have been on a quest for this power. You have been exploring God's power that comes through relationship with the Spirit of Christ. You studied the power that enables you to conquer habitual sinning and the self-serving attitude that leads you to selfish choices. You learned of the power that helps you through the trials of life that come your way to strengthen your faith and make you a better Christian. You were reminded of power to resist the temptations Satan sends to destroy you and your faith. You realized there is power to assist you in sharing your witness for Christ and in working in the Christian community to make new disciples for Him.

So how does God grant you this power? You receive it. Yes,

you can *receive* power for the life you've longed for. This power does not come your way through strenuous spiritual exercise. You neither earn it nor purchase it. As with so many of our other discoveries on this 40-day quest, this power can only be received as a gift from God's generous hand. Notice again our text for today: "You will *receive* power."

Read Acts 1:4-8. Jesus' disciples rode the emotional roller coaster of His last days of ministry, crucifixion, resurrection, and now parting words. As they said their last good-byes, Jesus left His disciples a promise. He'd told them about the Spirit prior to His crucifixion (John 14—17).

Now, the time arrived for them to meet Him personally. Jesus compared the Spirit's coming to a baptism, something like the water baptism of John the Baptist (Matt. 3:11-12). John preached a message of repentance. The Spirit's baptism would result in heart cleansing. Both baptisms are important; the Spirit's is superior to John's.

Jesus set the bar of anticipation high as He talked about such things as power, being internally filled with the Spirit, and being witnesses of Christ around the world. The power He talked about in verse 8 differed greatly from the power the disciples spoke of in verse 6. The disciples hoped Jesus would exercise political power; He envisioned spiritual power for His followers. Yes, His kingdom would come, but not through a political revolution. He had a far more subtle plan; He would bring about His kingdom through the disciples' personal witness given in the power of His Spirit.

The disciples couldn't grasp Jesus' big vision. They had no idea what He was talking about. They could tell from His description, though, that this baptism would be absolutely essential for their success with the mission He had given them to tackle once He left them (Matt. 28:19-20). No doubt, fear and uncertainty gripped their hearts at that moment. Jesus assured them that the Spirit's presence would make them adequate for the task.

Read Acts 2:1-4. We considered this passage on Day 5 in relationship to God's work with the first disciples of Jesus. We want to look at this story again today to consider its possibilities for us.

The birthday of the Church occurred on the Feast of Pentecost. No coincidence, just as Jesus' crucifixion at the Feast of Passover had been no coincidence. The timing of both events is significant in biblical and spiritual symbolism.

The Feast of Passover commemorated the Hebrew people's exodus from Egyptian bondage (Exod. 12:41-43). The death of Jesus brought the possibility for humanity's deliverance from sin's bondage. The Feast of Pentecost commemorated God giving the Hebrew people His Law (Lev. 23:15-16). The coming of the Spirit brought us the internal power and ability to live the way the Law originally intended for us to live.

Isn't it amazing how God works to teach us spiritual truths even in the timing of events like Christ's death and the Spirit's coming?

The connection between the giving of the Law in the Old Testament and the coming of the Holy Spirit in the New Testament does not end with timing. God's announcement of a spectacular event with bright light and loud sounds accompanied both. At the giving of the Law, God used thunder, lightning, a thick cloud, and a very loud trumpet blast (Exod. 19:16). At the coming of the Holy Spirit, God used a blast of wind, individual flames of fire, and a miraculous ability for Jesus' disciples to speak in languages they had never learned.

Each of the three symbols God used at the Spirit's coming held spiritual meaning. The wind reminds us of its ability to separate chaff from wheat (Matt. 3:12). The Spirit comes to blow away all that is unholy in our lives. The flames remind us of fire's ability to burn chaff and purge gold and silver from impurities (Mal. 3:2-4). The Spirit comes to purge our hearts of all that makes us less than God hopes for us to be. The miracle of languages reminds us of the call to communicate the good news of Jesus Christ to every person in his or her own tongue (Matt. 28:19-20).

The hardest part of a big event is usually the cleanup. Sometimes we're left with quite a mess. After the balloons and streamers are taken down, the trash gathered, and the place swept, we often look back on the scene and ask, "What really happened here?" We're looking for the continuing results or the long-term effect of the big event.

This same question can be asked about the Day of Pentecost in the lives of Jesus' disciples after the wind ceased, the fire died, and the spoken word fell silent. The Book of Acts tells the rest of the story; the gospel message began to spread across the entire world. Pentecost was more than a birthday celebration for the emerging Church. Disciples were springing up everywhere. The results lasted far beyond the cleanup. In fact, we're still tallying the results today. Pentecost launched a revolution, not politically speaking as the disciples envisioned, but in the hearts of Jesus' followers—both then and now. The power Jesus spoke of in Acts 1:8 changed us and our world forever.

There's no doubt about it. God has the power for the life you long for. He wants to give it to you. You must do what Jesus' disciples did: ask for His gift and wait for His response. Remember not to desire the gift over the Giver. The gift is a by-product of a close, personal relationship with God.

---

# DAY 33

**Remember:**

You can receive the power from God for the life you've longed for.

*You will receive power when the Holy Spirit comes on you (Acts 1:8).*

# DISCOVERY 5
## YOU CAN DEVELOP CHRISTLIKE CHARACTER.

## Memory Verse for the Week

*To them God has chosen to make known among the Gentiles the glorious riches of this mystery, which is Christ in you, the hope of glory* (Col. 1:27).

# DAY 34
# CHRIST IN YOU,
## PART 1

*To them God has chosen to make known among the Gentiles the glorious riches of this mystery, which is Christ in you, the hope of glory* (Col. 1:27).

FOR THE past month we've been on a quest to discover how we can live the life we long for. This quest has led us to four discoveries so far. We've learned we have a Guide for the life we long for. Our relationship with this Guide allows us to accept God's love, experience His purity, and receive His power for this life.

Now we're ready to set out on one last quest. This quest will point us in the direction of a Christlike character. Christianity has many unique features when compared to other world faiths. The most unique feature of them all is a close personal relationship with our God. We talk to Him in prayer much like other faiths talk to their gods. However, He talks back to us; that's unique! More than just talking to us, our God molds us over time to think and act as He does. We become like our God. That leads to the character development we want to explore for the next few days.

The Bible provides us with crystal-clear images into this discovery. Our text for today says Christ is in us. Paul tells us in Rom. 8:29 that God wants us "to be conformed to the likeness of his Son." Again, Paul says he is working with the Galatians "until Christ is formed in you" (Gal. 4:19). He goes on in 2 Cor. 3:18 to say that we "are being transformed into his

[Christ's] likeness with ever-increasing glory, which comes from the Lord, who is the Spirit."

God works with us during our lifetimes to develop a Christ-like character. The Taj Mahal wasn't built in a day. Your character won't take shape overnight either. What does that character look like? As we look at the life qualities of Christ, we begin to see what God wants to develop in us. Let's look at qualities Christ displayed in His earthly ministry.

1. *Jesus loved the Father first and foremost, then He loved us as an outgrowth of the Father's and Son's love for each other.*

Jesus' words and deeds throughout His earthly life evidenced those two priorities in His love life. He demonstrated daily what He proclaimed in His ministry. "'Love the Lord your God with all your heart and with all your soul and with all your mind.' This is the first and greatest commandment. And the second is like it: 'Love your neighbor as yourself.' All the Law and the Prophets hang on these two commandments" (Matt. 22:37-40).

2. *Jesus had a winsome personality.*

Crowds numbering in the thousands pressed Him. Something about His life and conversation attracted them. They wanted to hear what He had to say and see Him in action (John 6:1-2). People felt at ease in His presence. Many people, like Nicodemus, opened up and shared their hearts with Him (3:1-21).

3. *Jesus lived a life of humility.*

Jesus did not put himself down, rather He gave himself away to meet the needs of others. He even talked about being lowly in spirit as a virtue for us to emulate. "Take my yoke upon you and learn from me, for I am gentle and humble in heart, and you will find rest for your souls" (Matt. 11:29). Once His disciples argued among themselves about which of them was greater. Jesus illustrated the error of their thinking by placing a child among them and stressing the virtue of childlikeness (Matt. 18:1-5). When James and John sought to rule with Him in His coming kingdom, Jesus pointed out that those who want to rule over all must become humble servants of all (Mark 10:43-45). Then, at the Last Supper, He washed His disciples' feet as an example of humility (John 13:2-16).

4. *Jesus lived a balanced life.*

Jesus worked, rested, spent time with others, took time to be alone, socialized with both saints and sinners, and enjoyed the give and take of daily life. He was neither a workaholic nor a man of leisure. He stayed busy, but He knew when to stop and rest.

5. *Jesus had a sense of humor.*

Jesus wasn't always seriously preaching and teaching. He mixed a great deal of humor with His personal conversation and formal messages. He spoke of seeing a splinter while tripping over a large board (Matt. 7:3). He joked about tediously straining a gnat out of a drink, then swallowing a camel (23:24). Try to picture those images without laughing!

6. *Jesus had a heart of compassion and gave His hands to compassionate ministry.*

As He walked and talked with the crowds of people who followed Him, Jesus' heart reached out to their hurts and needs. Anyone who came to Jesus found a listening ear and an outstretched hand. He sympathized with people and did what He could to help them (8:14-17).

7. *Jesus lived a life of fairness.*

He defended His disciples when others wrongly accused them but also scolded them openly when they were wrong (Mark 2:23-24). For example, He criticized Peter when he rebuked Jesus for predicting His death but praised Peter for recognizing Jesus as the Christ, the Son of the living God (Matt. 16:13-23).

8. *Jesus was courteous.*

He spoke with dignity and respect to society's outcasts and

those with sinful pasts. A person's station in life did not impress Jesus. He treated the rich, poor, educated, uneducated, important, and disenfranchised all the same. Jesus, a Jewish male, conversed with the Samaritan female in a public place. Social convention never permitted this practice. At the end of the religious discussion, Jesus led her to a relationship with God (John 4:4-26). In His mind, everyone needed a relationship with His Father.

9. *Jesus was thoughtful.*

In the confusion of Jesus' arrest in the Garden of Gethsemane, Peter lashed out with his sword and cut off the right ear of the high priest's servant. Jesus touched the man's ear and miraculously healed him (Luke 22:50-51).

10. *Jesus paid compliments and showed appreciation.*

Jesus paid a high compliment to a sinful woman and created a social scene at the home of a Pharisee when the woman honored Jesus by anointing His feet with alabaster perfume and wiping them with her hair (7:36-50).

11. *Jesus did not attempt to create conflict with His enemies, but when it arose He did not run from it.*

The Pharisees, at one point in Jesus' ministry, prepared to do battle with Jesus, so He picked up and moved His ministry from Judea back through Samaria to Galilee (John 4:1-3). However, when the chief priests and teachers of the Law tried to trip Him up with a trick question, He stood up to them and refused to answer their question (Luke 20:1-8). On another occasion, Jesus publicly broke a manmade Sabbath rule to make a point with a Pharisee (14:1-4).

12. *Jesus did not contemplate His plight in life and feel sorry for himself.*

He lived with the shame and slander surrounding society's notion of His illegitimate birth. He acknowledged personal rejection by His hometown community. He lived with constant opposition from His enemies. His own brothers and sisters did not honor Him during His ministry. His own disciples did not understand Him most of the time. Yet, He did not assume a victim mentality, blame others, or feel sorry for himself (23:28).

Think about each of these qualities of Christ throughout the day and imagine ways the Father might make you more like His Son.

# DAY 34

**Remember:**

The Father wants to make you like His Son!

*Christ in you, the hope of glory* (Col. 1:27).

# DAY 35
# CHRIST IN YOU,
## PART 2

*To them God has chosen to make known among the Gentiles the glorious riches of this mystery, which is Christ in you, the hope of glory* (Col. 1:27).

WE BEGAN our study of Christlike character development yesterday. Today we will continue that study with the reminder that character development does not occur overnight. God takes a lifetime of growth and maturity to produce Christlike character in us. Let's pick up our list of qualities where we left off yesterday.

13. *Jesus was not vindictive and did not retaliate when others treated Him wrongly.*

He urged us to turn the other cheek to wrongdoers, give to those who rob us, and go the second mile with those who impose on our kindness (Matt. 5:38-41).

14. *Jesus did not need to make a name for himself.*

He preached, taught, and healed in the midst of all who came to Him, but He never attempted to create fame or fortune for himself as an outgrowth of His successful ministry (12:11-16). In fact, He actually sought to keep His popularity from growing so as not to shorten His time of public ministry (16:20).

15. *Jesus expressed strong emotion and indignation when the occasion called for it.*

Jesus did not get angry over selfish concerns or become self-defensive over personal attacks, but He did react strongly at times. For example, He created quite a scene in the Temple area over the money changers and dove sellers (21:12-13). He also became upset when His disciples tried to keep children away from His ministry (Mark 10:13-16).

16. *Jesus showed great courage throughout His life.*

He faced the frontal attacks of Satan during 40 days of temptation. He courageously began His public ministry in the shadow of His popular cousin John the Baptist's ministry. He publicly opposed the human traditional laws that were inhumane and ungodly. He countered the religious leaders in their errors. He called sin by its real name and pointed to it in the lives of those to whom He spoke. He refused to lower himself to the demands of the people to crown Him as their king. He courageously accepted the Father's plan for His life even though it meant going to the Cross.

17. *Jesus had a clear mission and purpose for His life.*

He had this mission and purpose clearly in place by the time He first visited the Temple at the age of 12 (Luke 2:49). He carried this vision with Him throughout His earthly ministry (4:18). He worked daily with a sense of urgency. He envisioned the harvest of souls at hand and did all He could to bring that harvest to His Father (John 4:34-35).

18. *Jesus lived with eternity's values in view.*

Jesus kept His feet firmly planted on the ground, so to speak, but He never lost sight of heaven's view. Every event in His earthly life, from the beginning of His ministry to the Cross, gave Him opportunity to show how to respond in light of eternity's value system. He never surrendered to the immediate at the expense of the eternal. Every word He said, every miracle He performed, all somehow related to God's eternal purposes. He maintained a strong patriotism toward the homeland of His true citizenship—the kingdom of God.

19. *Jesus realized and accepted His human limitations.*

When His body grew weary, He stopped and rested. He slept after difficult days of ministry. When His nervous system reached the point of exhaustion from the press of the crowds,

He withdrew from society and spent time alone. When He saw His ministry growing, He delegated tasks to His disciples rather than trying to do everything himself. When the burden grew heavy in the Garden of Gethsemane, He sought His disciples' help in carrying the load.

20. *Jesus always sought to do the will of His Father.*

He demonstrated this perspective when He was 12 years old (Luke 2:49) and carried it with Him to the Garden of Gethsemane (Matt. 26:39, 42). Obedience to the Father's work and plan remained the driving force of His life. More than anything, He wanted to see His Father's will accomplished (John 4:34; 6:38). In everything He did, Jesus saw himself as an ambassador for the Father.

21. *Jesus lived in constant communion with His Father.*

Prayer remained a constant source of strength for Jesus. He bathed the beginning of His ministry in prayer (Luke 6:12). He spent extended seasons of prayer after particularly taxing events, such as the feeding of the thousands (Mark 6:46). He called attention to the importance of prayer before performing miracles (John 11:41).

22. *Jesus depended on the Holy Spirit for constant spiritual strength and encouragement.*

The Spirit filled Jesus to adequately prepare Him for His battle with Satan's temptation (Luke 4:1). Everything Jesus accomplished in His earthly life He accomplished through the power of God's Spirit working through Him. This became clear as He came to the end of His life on earth and prayed that His disciples and those of us who would believe later might have that same Spirit at work within (John 17:1-26).

23. *Jesus lived a life of service.*

Whether ministering to the multitudes, the 70 close followers, or the 12 disciples, Jesus found ways to give himself away in service to those who needed Him. He placed their needs ahead of His own. He left us an admonition to selfless service in the parable of the sheep and the goats. The focal point of that story rings in our ears to this day, "The King will reply, 'I tell you the truth, whatever you did for one of the least of these brothers of mine, you did for me'" (Matt. 25:40). Following the washing of His disciples' feet, Jesus said, "I have set you an example that you should do as I have done for you" (John 13:15).

24. *Jesus submitted himself to suffering on our behalf.*

The sufferings of Jesus are clearly documented throughout the New Testament Gospels. Paul reminds us of our part in sharing this ministry of suffering. "For just as the sufferings of Christ flow over into our lives, so also through Christ our comfort overflows" (2 Cor. 1:5). Paul's heart cried out to participate with Christ in this way. "I want to know Christ and the power of his resurrection and the fellowship of sharing in his sufferings, becoming like him in his death" (Phil. 3:10). Peter also realized the need for us to follow Christ's example. "To this you were called, because Christ suffered for you, leaving you an example, that you should follow in his steps" (1 Pet. 2:21).

25. *Jesus submitted himself to death on the Cross to accomplish our salvation.*

Christ's death on the Cross opened the way for us to live in vital relationship with the Father. It also led to the formation of the Church, the Body of Christ on earth, which carries on His work until He returns. Christ's crucifixion symbolizes the importance of our own daily crucifixion to self-will and self-denial (Gal. 2:20).

Further, it reminds us that if we live and witness for Christ, we will pay the price along with Him. "Now I rejoice in what was suffered for you, and I fill up in my flesh what is still lacking in regard to Christ's afflictions, for the sake of his body, which is the church" (Col. 1:24). We must always remember the words of Jesus to His disciples, "If anyone would come after me, he must deny himself and take up his cross and follow me" (Matt. 16:24).

Look back over the list of qualities or virtues discussed yesterday and today. God wants to form these in you as you grow in Him. Resist the tendency to make a list of these character qualities and grade your daily performance. If you fall into that trap, you'll live in bondage to performance. Just live for God and seek His ways. Growth in Christlikeness will follow as naturally as flowers in April.

# DAY 35

**Remember:**

You can become like Christ!

*Christ in you, the hope of glory* (Col. 1:27).

# A HOLY AND PLEASING OFFERING

*Therefore, I urge you, brothers, in view of God's mercy, to offer your bodies as living sacrifices, holy and pleasing to God—this is your spiritual act of worship. Do not conform any longer to the pattern of this world, but be transformed by the renewing of your mind. Then you will be able to test and approve what God's will is—his good, pleasing and perfect will* (Rom. 12:1-2).

THE CHILDREN'S STORY "Hansel and Gretel" tells about a boy and girl who dropped bread crumbs along their path through the woods so they could retrace their steps and find the way home. Too bad they didn't have a global positioning system! Bread crumbs are so low-tech.

We have been using something like bread crumbs along the path of our quest over the past 35 days. The time has arrived for us to trace back across some of the ideas we have discussed and make some important connections. These connections are essential for bringing our quest to a successful conclusion.

On Day 3 we talked about the need for growth in our spiritual lives. Growth is a necessary quality of life. The next day we focused on a subtle spiritual hindrance that arrests our growth. Day 5 reminded us that Jesus' disciples received a radical transformation with the coming of the Spirit of Christ at Pentecost.

Something happened that day that empowered the disciples for a lifetime of spiritual growth and ministry. Each of the discovery quests—for guidance, love, purity, power, and Christlike character—requires us to give something to God and to receive something from Him.

The common experience of saints down through the ages has been an awareness of a remaining hindrance to further spiritual progress. No outward sin; just an uncertain gnawing for something more. This awareness usually takes the form of an internal battle with self, such as Paul described in Gal. 5:16-26. In summary he said, "For the sinful nature desires what is contrary to the Spirit, and the Spirit what is contrary to the sinful nature. They are in conflict with each other, so that you do not do what you want" (v. 17).

The battle may be self-centeredness in the form of self-seeking, self-assertion, self-indulgence, self-sufficiency, or self-will —all ways we prefer ourselves over God and others. It's not that we do not wish to please God; we do. Our problem involves wanting the best of both worlds—have what God wants and what we want at the same time. We know we cannot have it both ways.

Once we pinpoint the self-centeredness, we realize it must be replaced with Christ-centeredness. We confess our need to God and surrender ourselves completely to His will. The old-timers called it "dying out to self." They did not mean self-extinction or psychological suicide; rather they meant self-preference replaced with God-preference. After full surrender comes faith in God to change us. We trust God to accept our consecration and fill us more completely with His Holy Spirit. The Spirit entered our lives when we accepted Christ; now we are inviting Him to take charge of our control center.

Today's text describes our consecration. Read Rom. 12:1-2. Paul spent the first 11 chapters of his letter to the Romans familiarizing the reader with a line of thinking that begins to take practical application in chapter 12. The theological discussions in the earlier portions of the book as well as this practical application all center around making Jesus the Lord of our lives. So, we must believe the right doctrines about Christ, think correctly about our Christian faith, and live holy lives that honor God. Paul now begins to tell us how to position ourselves for successful holy living.

Paul reminds us to begin our consecration by remembering God's mercy in not condemning us in our sins but in giving us another chance to live for Him. God's mercy becomes our motivation for consecration. In light of His mercy toward us, how should we respond? We should respond by offering our bodies as living sacrifices back to Him. The imagery of Old Testament sacrifices are brought to mind when worshipers brought live animals to the altar. But before the ritual ended, the priest took the animals' lives. They were no longer of earthly use since they died in the process of the sacrifice.

Paul says we should willingly place our bodies on the sacrificial altar. Paul intends more than just dedication of our physical bodies; he implies the dedication of our entire being. That is, we dedicate the physical, spiritual, emotional, and psychological parts of ourselves. God will not take our physical lives in the process; we will become living sacrifices. In other words, we consecrate our lives to God and His service, then go on living.

Paul offers another window into this imagery through the sacrifice Jesus made for us on the Cross. That sacrifice cost Jesus His physical life. As His disciples, we should identify with Him in His consecration to the Father. Paul wrote in Rom. 6:1-5 of our identifying with Christ in His death and resurrection through water baptism. In this ritual we die with Christ; God raises us to new life in Him.

Today's Scripture lesson identifies us again with Christ. He willingly lay down to be nailed to the Cross. We, too, should willingly offer our lives back to God. Our consecration differs from Christ's in that we go on living following our act of dedication. His consecration required His life. In Matt. 10:24 Jesus reminded us, "A student is not above his teacher, nor a servant above his master." He climbed upon the sacrificial altar; we must follow.

Some claim that in Romans Paul is admonishing prospective converts to the Christian faith. Thus, they say, this consecration occurs at the time of a believer's conversion. The word "holy" in the middle of verse 1 indicates otherwise. Paul addresses believers who have already been declared holy in light of the fact that they have invited Christ into their hearts. They are now, as holy ones, to offer themselves on the altar of sacrifice. This response pleases God. It is a response similar to the one Jesus experienced when He healed 10 lepers. One returned to thank Him as His praise response to God (Luke 17:11-19). We praise God with our consecration.

In the last part of verse 1, Paul calls our consecration an act of worship. Worship requires that we give something to God. We usually think of giving Him our words of praise, our prayers, or our songs. But, do those gifts really cost us anything? You might say it costs us time and energy in going to a church building to offer them. Is that really much of a price to pay?

On one occasion during His reign as king of Israel, David worshiped God by making a special sacrifice to Him. He gave us a principle that remains an important reminder to us today. He said, "I will not sacrifice to the LORD my God burnt offerings that cost me nothing" (2 Sam. 24:24). Ultimately, true worship always costs us something. Paul says in the last phrase of verse 1 that God is calling us to a type of worship that will cost us everything.

Look again at Rom. 12:2. When a person dies, he or she no longer has obligations to the law. A dead person no longer files income tax or registers to vote. In Paul's mind, believers who have offered themselves to God as living sacrifices are as good as dead while they live in this world. Therefore, they no longer think like the world thinks or value as the world values. They do not define reality the way most people define it. They do not need society to prescribe for them the latest in fashion, entertainment, or lifestyle choices. They march to the beat of a different drummer and have their sights set on different goals in life.

Believers consecrate themselves to God as living sacrifices and something miraculous happens. Their values are different from the world's values; God radically transforms their lives. At times, the transformation occurs so slowly they hardly perceive it, but it is real nonetheless. The transformation gives these consecrated believers the mind of Christ. Paul said in 1 Cor. 2:16, "But we have the mind of Christ." We find ourselves placing a high value on the things Christ highly values. We lose interest in the things of the world that Christ tells us will pass away.

Offering yourself as a living sacrifice and developing the mind of Christ will produce remarkable changes in your life. You will discern a sense of God's will. You will not follow His will begrudgingly or from a sense of obligation. Rather, you will discover that it is "good, pleasing and perfect" as Paul describes it. It is good because it comes from God; it is pleasing as you apply it to your life; and it is perfect, not in the sense of perfect performance but in the sense of completely dedicated to God. God accepts the offer of your life and rewards you with an indescribable sense of His pleasure with you. What a priceless benefit of consecrated living!

It may be easy to say you are offering yourself to God. But is it easy to do? What if God requests too much of your time and money? What if He asks you to change careers or move, like He asked Abraham? What if you end up halfway around the world? What then? *Well, you say, I'm really serious about consecrating myself fully to Him. Whatever He asks, I'm willing to do. I'm just a glove for His hand to fill.*

# Day 36

**Remember:**

We must offer ourselves to God as living sacrifices.

*I urge you, brothers, in view of God's mercy, to offer your bodies as living sacrifices, holy and pleasing to God—this is your spiritual act of worship* (Rom. 12:1).

# ACCEPTING GOD'S GIFT

*May God himself, the God of peace, sanctify you through and through. May your whole spirit, soul and body be kept blameless at the coming of our Lord Jesus Christ. The one who calls you is faithful and he will do it* (1 Thess. 5:23-24).

MY HIGH SCHOOL literature teacher required us to read Charles Dickens' book *Great Expectations.* It had a profound impact on the way I think. The book tells the story of Philip Pirrip, nicknamed Pip, who encountered Abel Magwitch, an escaped convict, early in his life. Magwitch worked quietly behind the scenes as a secret benefactor throughout Pip's life to provide him with resources and opportunities that elevated him into high society. Much later, Pip looked back over the path his life had taken and saw the unmistakable hand of his secret benefactor.

Human nature causes us to think instinctively in terms of being self-sufficient and self-made. Nearly everyone has a story to illustrate an example of how "I did it all by myself." We like to think in terms of the rugged individualist or the self-made person. That's seldom the case, however. More often than not, we succeed because of a team effort or a friend or relative working quietly behind the scenes to assist in our accomplishments. When I was a child, my parents paved a wide path for my success in school. My entire adult life has been blessed with my wife, Sue, working tirelessly to assist me. I'm not a self-made person; you're probably not either.

The same is true of spiritual success. As we have said many times in the book, God gives us many benefits. He works quietly behind the scenes to assist in our success. He gives us salvation, for starters, along with numerous other benefits along life's path. Yesterday we talked about consecration; today we look at God's gift of sanctification. We do not earn or deserve sanctification any more than we earn or deserve new birth.

Sanctification and related words—"sanctify," "holy," "holiness"—are found in the Bible more than 1,100 times. Scripture repeats the concept often. In both of the biblical languages of Old Testament Hebrew and New Testament Greek, words such as "holiness" and "sanctification" are used somewhat interchangeably. They do, however, convey different meanings in English.

"Holiness" comes from an old English word also translated "whole," "health," or "hallow." It refers to being whole, in good health, or holy. Basically, "sanctification" refers to the total, lifelong process of becoming holy. It's all God does in us to restore our hearts to the way He created us to be. The moment at which God gifts us with sanctification refers to a particular point in time when we consecrate self fully to God and offer up the stronghold of self-preference. So "holiness" is a broad term; "sanctification" is more focused.

Yesterday we concluded that our self-seeking, self-willed, self-sufficient ways must go. A new availability to all God wants for me replaces the *self*isms. Thus, holiness is the attitude of our souls and characterization of the lifestyle that results from God's sanctification.

In preparation for our Scripture focus, read 1 Thess. 4:1-8. Every believer must ultimately decide who he or she will please—God or self. Paul urges us in verse 1 to seek to please God in all we do. This is not just a suggestion made by a minister; it's a command coming from the authority of Jesus him-self (John 8:29). Verse 3 zeros in on one of the central themes of the Book of Thessalonians: "It is God's will that you should be sanctified."

A believer will often pray for God's will in relation to the choice of a mate, an education, a career, or a location to settle down. All important choices. No choice is more important, how-ever, than seeking God's will for a clean and pure heart. None of the other choices will bring the satisfaction you seek in life if you do not first have a heart with a single focus toward God.

Paul first says our sanctification manifests itself in sexual purity. The Thessalonian Christians lived in a society plagued by sexual immorality, much like our society. The prevailing cul-ture condoned all sorts of sexual activity that the Bible con-demned as sinful. Paul urged the Thessalonians to resist all temptations to blend in with their culture and adopt its lax moral practices. He warned to never become comfortable with the world's moral standards and to always remember God called them to a higher standard.

Verse 4 reminds us of an important responsibility: self-con-trol. God may not take us out of temptation's reach, but He ex-pects us to learn to say no to temptation. Unbelievers live under the control of their passionate lusts, surrendering to tempta-tion. God expects better of believers. Holy living also mandates "and that in this matter no one should wrong his brother or take advantage of him. The Lord will punish men for all such sins, as we have already told you and warned you" (v. 6).

Verse 3 tells us it is God's will for us to be sanctified. Verse 7 says God calls us to be holy. And verse 8 says, "Therefore, he who rejects this instruction does not reject man but God, who gives you his Holy Spirit." The key to both God's will and God's call for our lives: God's gift of His Spirit. The tense of the verb indicates this is not a one-time gift but a continual, daily giving of His Spirit.

Our text for today is 1 Thess. 5:23-24. Chapters 4 and 5 of 1 Thessalonians are full of admonitions of things to do and not do in order to exemplify holiness. Here, he suggests the secret that makes holiness possible in our lives. We cannot discipline ourselves into such living. We simply cannot live up to the standard under our own power. We need the God of peace to do a work in our lives that will enable us to live up to His will and call for us. In 1 Thess. 5:23 we are reminded of the same truth found in 4:8, that is, sanctification is not something we do for ourselves; God does it. We receive God's gift by faith.

"To sanctify" means to set apart for God. God set apart the tabernacle and the Temple as places of worship in the Old Testament. He also set apart the instruments of worship. In the New Testament, it is believers who are sanctified rather than places or things. God sets us apart for himself, but with an added dimension. He cleanses and purifies our hearts and places His Spirit within us to enable us to live the lives to which He calls us.

"Blameless" does not imply "faultless," as we discussed on Day 21. The word "blame" comes from the same word as "blaspheme," which means to deny that God is God. To be blameless is to be innocent of wrongdoing. In this context, it means to honor God as Lord of our lives. Faultless, on the other hand, means to be without error, flawless—perfect. Our hearts and motives can be blameless before God even though our actions may not always be perfect.

The verb "sanctify" in 5:23 differs significantly from the word "gives" in 4:8. In 4:8 Paul speaks of a continual, daily giving of His Spirit rather than a one-time gift. Think of a child receiving lunch money each day from Mom. In 5:23 Paul calls for a decisive action at a point in time. Think of receiving a birthday present from your parent. So, we see that God accepts our consecration, yesterday's topic, by giving us the gift of sanctification at a moment in time. He also places His Spirit in us on a daily basis. Hence, we experience both a moment-in-time experience and a daily process of growth toward maturity.

God doesn't just affect our religious nature or our psychological nature. He affects every part of our being: spirit, soul, and body. God touches every part of our spiritual and physical being and sustains us. How long does He sustain us? Until the new wears off our spiritual experience or until we mature in our faith? No, He sustains us all the way to the second coming of Christ.

Paul wants to make sure we understand the source for fulfilling this call to holy living, so he reminds us of it again in verse 24. God calls; God is faithful; He will do it. Yes, my commitment to Him is important. Yes, my self-discipline is also important. However, God's gift of His Spirit and His sanctification are the real reasons we can live holy lives.

Paul's letter to the believers at Thessalonica reminds us of important spiritual truths. God calls us to live holy lives. His will and plan for our lives calls us to sanctification. This comes as God's gift. He sanctifies in a moment and gives His Spirit daily for a lifetime of growth in sanctification.

# DAY 37

## Remember:

Our quest will succeed only after we receive God's gift of sanctification.

*May God himself, the God of peace, sanctify you through and through. May your whole spirit, soul and body be kept blameless at the coming of our Lord Jesus Christ* (1 Thess. 5:23).

# GROWING IN THE SPIRIT OF CHRIST

*For this reason, since the day we heard about you, we have not stopped praying for you and asking God to fill you with the knowledge of his will through all spiritual wisdom and understanding. And we pray this in order that you may live a life worthy of the Lord and may please him in every way: bearing fruit in every good work, growing in the knowledge of God, being strengthened with all power according to his glorious might so that you may have great endurance and patience, and joyfully giving thanks to the Father, who has qualified you to share in the inheritance of the saints in the kingdom of light* (Col. 1:9-12).

GOD grants you the incredible gift of spiritual life when you accept Christ as your personal Savior. But, you can't be a passive recipient of that gift and grow in Christlike character. Character growth doesn't happen while you sleep or watch television. God expects you to roll up your sleeves and do your part to exercise, grow, and mature. This passage of Scripture reminds us that we need to be continually filled with an awareness of God's will. As we intentionally study God's Word and purposefully participate in the spiritual exercises that develop us, we grow in spiritual wisdom and understanding.

The spiritual journey may begin in a rush of feeling and emotion; these will eventually subside. One never finds a solid foundation for his or her spiritual journey in feeling and emotion. Feeling and emotion come and go. You and I must move on to spiritual wisdom and understanding for solid growth in Christlike character.

Such wisdom and understanding lead to responsible living. Our faith bears fruit in the daily conduct of godly living that pleases God. Wisdom and understanding lead to good works. We always live out what we believe. That's why it's important to believe biblical truth. Growth in wisdom, understanding, and good works lead to growth in our knowledge of God as well as growth in Christlike character.

We, in turn, find new strength from God for endurance, patience, and joyful thanksgiving: all signs of Christian maturity. Paul reminds us again of our heavenly inheritance at the culmination of our spiritual journey. From now until that day, we live as citizens of the kingdom of light. Light symbolizes holiness, righteousness, truth, and life. All belong to us because we belong to Him.

Take a moment and look at your study material for Days 34 to 38. On Days 34 and 35 we reviewed the characteristics of Jesus' life that offer goals for us to develop Christlike character. We learned we can't develop these characteristics simply by trying harder to live virtuously or by our own determined willpower. God works in our hearts to create these qualities in us. God accomplishes decisive, character-building work in us only after we consecrate ourselves totally to Him. After we offer ourselves as living sacrifices, He fills us with the Spirit of Christ. Once we offer ourselves and He accepts our offer, we enter a clear path to a lifetime of growth and development in Christlike character.

The list of qualities from the life of Christ from Days 34 and 35 in no way exhaust the many aspects of Christ we can emulate. There are others: patience, sympathy, frankness, cooperation, discernment of truth, nonconformity, reconciliation, and peace. Peter and Paul have given us lists of Christian virtues we should seek in our lives.

Peter reminds us of additional virtues: "For this very reason, make every effort to add to your faith goodness; and to goodness, knowledge; and to knowledge, self-control; and to self-control, perseverance; and to perseverance, godliness; and to godliness, brotherly kindness; and to brotherly kindness, love" (2 Pet. 1:5-7). And in Rom. 5:3-5, Paul: "Not only so, but we also rejoice in our sufferings, because we know that suffering produces perseverance; perseverance, character; and character, hope. And hope does not disappoint us, because God has poured out his love into our hearts by the Holy Spirit, whom he has given us."

Now that we have a list of growth goals, how do we go about incorporating them into our lives? On Day 3 we listed some growth strategies. To quickly review, we said believers grow through:

- Prayer
- Bible reading
- Meditation
- Corporate worship
- The Lord's Supper
- Christian fellowship
- Fasting
- Listening to Christian music
- Reading Christian literature
- Practicing the presence of God every day
- Disciplining your life to make it consistent with your commitment to Christ
- Learning to cope with life's daily circumstances

- Committing to the Lord your past failures, appetites, weaknesses, temptations, the failures of others, and situations you cannot change
- Opening all of your life to Kingdom priorities

Paul discussed character development from another angle in Eph. 4:11-13. This passage reveals God's plan and provision for spiritual growth and development. Verse 11 lists the workers God calls to instruct and encourage His followers. Everyone has an assignment in Christ's work. Pay particular attention to the reasons in the following verses that God assigns each of us a task:

- To prepare us for works of service (v. 12a)
- To build up the Body of Christ (v. 12b)
- To bring unity in the faith (v. 13a)
- To bring unity in the knowledge of Jesus (v. 13b)
- To bring spiritual maturity (v. 13c)

Can you see God's plan to enrich our lives personally as well as to enrich the community of faith? We grow as we minister to one another, and the community of faith grows as well. All are strengthened and helped as we develop individually and corporately. In the process, we become more like Christ.

The purpose of this plan is to bring us to a common belief, a common Savior, and a common model for our spiritual maturity. The Spirit of Christ grows a Christlike character in you and builds His kingdom at the same time.

Read Eph. 4:14-16. Paul presents the alternative to God's plan and goal for you. God doesn't want you to be a spiritual baby, an infant who will never grow out of the "baby stage." He doesn't want you to be a little life raft floating aimlessly on an open sea.

These are the images of believers who do not move on to Christian maturity. The winds that blow them around are the false teachings that blow through society, media, and sometimes even the church. False teachings can blow through unintentionally. That is, sometimes people simply throw out false ideas for consideration without a specific target in mind. At other times false teachers intentionally target certain believers with the specific purpose of attempting to lead them astray. Spiritual growth and maturity will insulate believers from these pitfalls.

If God has His way in us, we will speak and hear the truth, and we will grow in Christ. Christ works like glue holding believers together to form His Body on earth. The last portion of this passage still has us growing. We build each other up in love; we each do our part to help and support one another. Christian maturity brings spiritual unity to the Body of Christ.

Passages of Scripture such as the ones we've studied today remind us that God does not want us to allow spiritual complacency in our lives. We must never relax our efforts toward further growth by deciding that we have arrived spiritually. Right standing with God does not exempt us from the need for further spiritual growth. We must balance our thinking between satisfaction in what Christ accomplished for us on the Cross and a hunger to press on to a deeper walk with God. We can relax our efforts only after we step through the gates of our heavenly home.

# DAY 38

## Remember:
The Spirit of Christ wants to grow a Christlike character in you.

*For this reason, since the day we heard about you, we have not stopped praying for you and asking God to fill you with the knowledge of his will through all spiritual wisdom and understanding* (Col. 1:9).

# LIFE IN THE SPIRIT OF CHRIST

*Therefore, there is now no condemnation for those who are in Christ Jesus, because through Christ Jesus the law of the Spirit of life set me free from the law of sin and death* (Rom. 8:1-2).

THIS WEEK'S quest has taken us through the steps necessary to develop Christlike character. First, we set Christ's example as our model. Then, we consecrate ourselves completely to God. Next, we receive His gift of sanctification. From that point on, we move from one growth cycle to another for the rest of our lives. Yesterday we studied a variety of strategies for developing Christlike character.

Today we will think about the many choices we make daily that shape life in the Spirit of Christ. If you have heard that God quantum-leaps you to Christlike maturity in one moment with one prayer, you have been misled. Yes, a decision to step down from the throne of self-sovereignty can be made in a moment. Yes, God accepts our consecration in a moment. However, the test of our resolve to make Christ Lord of all is validated daily with every choice. Life in the Spirit of Christ may have a memorable, starting-block moment, but the race you will run with Him is lifelong.

The word "therefore" that begins verse 1 in today's scripture refers back to the condemnation of the Law explored in Rom. 7. Christ took our place on the Cross; *therefore* He freed us from sin. Christ made us "at one" with the Father by covering our sins with His blood. We don't need to wait for death to bring deliverance from the bondage of sin. That deliverance becomes a present reality as we walk in the Spirit.

HE
FORGIVES
AND
FORGETS.

The key to understanding today's passage lies at the end of verse 1. The incredible freedom Paul speaks of requires you to choose daily the way you think, value, and live. You have two alternatives to choose from several times a day. One lives life after the flesh; the other lives life after the Spirit.

Read Rom. 8:2-9. This section shows the clear difference between life in the flesh and life in the Spirit of Christ. Paul refers to the flesh more than 12 times and the Spirit 16 times in this chapter of Romans. Rather than studying this section verse by verse, note Paul's offered between flesh and Spirit. Here are Paul's teachings on the two ways of living:

1. Two preferences (8:1, 8-9)
   a. In Christ Jesus: We are in Christ; He is in us. The Spirit brings the living presence of Christ not just *to* us but *in* us. You are united with Him in a mystical connection that brings daily communion between your spirit and His Spirit. Your spirit is not absorbed by His so as to nullify your personhood or cancel your freewill. Hence, you still make choices and think your own thoughts. The difference centers on your will preferring God's will to the point that His will becomes the very oxygen you breathe.
   b. In the flesh: The Bible uses flesh in three ways: (1) our bodies, (2) the human point of view, and (3) the

carnal nature of humanity that prefers self over God. Paul intends the third way in this passage of Scripture. The flesh represents a world that makes no attempt at pleasing or preferring God. It does what it wants, when it wants, and in the manner it wants. It follows whims of imagination and seeks its own happiness over other priorities.

2. Two walks (8:1, 4-5, 9)

   a. Spiritual walk: This walk is in step with the music of God's value system. Self-will falls along the roadside as the will and preference of God mark out the path. Sometimes this path runs totally counter to what we might choose for ourselves, but never mind. We want God's will so clearly that preferences we might have for ourselves don't seem that important in light of His plans for us.

   b. Fleshly walk: This walk is in step with the music of one's own value system. Self-will, self-seeking, and self-gratification mark the path for this walk. Sometimes the path goes over other people's backs, feelings, or well-being, but no matter; self-preference always carries the most authority in marking out this trail. The intention may not be to totally disregard God's ways, just not to let His ways have influence over my own ways.

3. Two laws (8:2)

   a. The law of the Spirit of life: This law comes not from a rule book or court bench but from the heart of Christ. It guides our thinking, feelings, actions, and attitudes. It's not so much a list of dos and don'ts as it is boundary lines of the relationship we have with God. That love relationship with God causes us to long for His ways, as taught to us by Christ's Spirit.

    *b.* The law of death: This law comes from Satan. It tells you, "Do what you please." It's a law that disregards all law. Think what you want to think. Do whatever you want to do. Make yourself happy. The problem with this law? It leads straight into the jaws of death.

4. Two powers (8:3-4)

    *a.* The power of Christ: Christ became our representative on the Cross. By His sacrifice we now have full remission for our sins. In God's eyes, it's just as if we'd never sinned in the first place. There's a big difference between God forgiving—but remembering—our sins and God forgiving and forgetting our sins. He forgives and forgets. Christ's power creates a new heart toward God and a new start with Him. Amazing power!

    *b.* The power of the Ten Commandments: This law tells us we must follow every regulation precisely to please God. However, it's humanly impossible to keep every regulation precisely. So when we fail or fall short, this law condemns us. It offers no power to succeed or further hope that we can ever meet its demands. Like a task master who cannot be pleased, it tells us we're wrong but offers no plan for correcting our way.

5. Two loyalties (8:5)

    *a.* Loyalty to the Spirit: This loyalty subjects us to the directives of the Spirit. It aims us toward God's will and preferences. Our desires fall subject to God's holy, pure, and good desires for us. It's not that we long to do one thing but force ourselves to do something else. It's that our desires conform to His to the point that, more than anything else in the world, we want what He wants. Our pleasure is to do His pleasure.

    *b.* Loyalty to the flesh: This loyalty subjects us to the

powerful whims of our desires, our addictions, and our passions. We become slaves to every drive that enters our minds. We obey it not because we think it is best for us, but because we cannot resist it. Loyalty to the flesh defies reason. It needs no other argument than "because I want to."

6. Two destinies (8:6-7)

    *a.* Life is quite ironic. Jesus said to save your life, you lose it (Matt. 16:25). So, when you surrender your will, preferences, desires, hopes, dreams, plans, wishes, body, soul, and spirit to God's Spirit, rather than losing your life, you actually gain life to the fullest. There's no need to wait for the end of your journey on earth to enjoy eternal life. Life lived in the Spirit gives you the joys and benefits of eternal life right now.

    *b.* Death ends in total destruction. The final stage of addiction brings total bondage. The final stage of self-seeking brings total selfishness. The final stage of the life of the flesh brings physical, spiritual, psychological, and emotional death.

Read Rom. 8:10-17. Paul outlines the glorious benefits of choosing life in the Spirit:

- The Spirit of Christ dwelling in your heart (v. 10)
- Physical resurrection from the dead (v. 11)
- Adoption into the family of God (vv. 14-15)
- The witness of God's Spirit to your spirit (v. 16)
- Joint-heirs with Christ (v. 17*a*)
- Glorification in heaven (v. 17*b*)

Words cannot describe the incredible reward awaiting those who decide to live life on God's terms—life in the Spirit of Christ. You validate your consecration and affirm your sanctification in daily choices as you continue to live out your resolve to make Christ Lord of all!

# DAY 39

**Remember:**

We live life in the Spirit of Christ every day through a thousand daily choices.

*Through Christ Jesus the law of the Spirit of life set me free from the law of sin and death* (Rom. 8:2).

# A LIFESTYLE OF SERVICE

*But he said to me, "My grace is sufficient for you, for my power is made perfect in weakness." Therefore I will boast all the more gladly about my weaknesses, so that Christ's power may rest on me. That is why, for Christ's sake, I delight in weaknesses, in insults, in hardships, in persecutions, in difficulties. For when I am weak, then I am strong* (2 Cor. 12:9-10).

YOUR ATTENTION on this 40-day quest has focused primarily on a personal spiritual journey and your involvement in the community of faith. We've talked about intimate heart issues and the value system used to determine priorities in life. We've talked about the need to consecrate everything to God and receive the gift of His sanctification. However, the quest cannot be complete until we focus attention away from ourselves and onto others and their needs.

Your spiritual life will become self-absorbed and short-sighted if you think only of yourself and your spiritual progress with God. Yesterday we looked briefly at the words of Jesus: "For whoever wants to save his life will lose it, but whoever loses his life for me will find it" (Matt. 16:25). Life in the Spirit of Christ involves giving your life away in service to others. Serving others is as vital to spiritual growth as praying or reading your Bible. Let's look at Paul's example of a lifestyle of service.

Paul met Christ on the Damascus Road (Acts 9:1-9). Paul became a lifelong disciple, committing himself wholly to following the will of God. As a result, Paul found himself in many less-than-desirable circumstances. However, he willingly endured those circumstances because they followed from his choice.

Read Paul's testimony in 2 Cor. 11:23-33. In answering his critics, Paul gives us a bit of his remarkable biography. Notice his résumé: hard work, prison, severe floggings, beatings with a rod, stoned, shipwrecked, adrift on an open sea, constantly on the move, dangerous river crossings, in danger from bandits, in danger from enemies, hard labor, toil, sleeplessness, hunger, thirst, exposure to cold, nakedness, church administration, and escape from death plots.

This sounds like a list of things to avoid. Who wants to live a life this hard? Paul presents this brief biographical sketch not to brag or seek pity but, as he says in verses 30-31, to offer praise to God for meeting him at the point of his weakness with strength to endure. Paul illustrates in living color the mind-set of service and ministry. God stationed Paul strategically in the thick of the battle, but He resourced him for that assignment as well.

Paul reminds us that serving God does not promise a flower-lined, easy path. But following God in radical discipleship produces a great sense of fulfillment and satisfaction even in the midst of trying circumstances. A part of the cost of following Christ, as He urges us to do in Luke 14:26-35, is that God's call may require extreme dedication and sacrifice. One whose heart is totally sold out to God stands ready to follow Him even on the difficult paths.

Paul teaches in 2 Cor. 12:7-8 a key principle of service and ministry: "To keep me from becoming conceited because of these surpassingly great revelations, there was given me a thorn in my flesh, a messenger of Satan, to torment me. Three times I pleaded with the Lord to take it away from me." That is, in the midst of very difficult circumstances, we can experience the blessing of God to the point that we wouldn't want life to be any other way. Paul did not suffer from delusions or denial; he was fully aware of the difficulty of his circumstances. In fact, he prayed adamantly for God to remove some of his difficulties. Rather than removing the difficulties, God promised Paul an extra measure of grace.

Paul reminds us in verse 7 that, as strange as it sounds, these difficulties can actually be seen as gifts that God allows. God's not the primary giver of the difficulties; Satan gets that credit. However, God finds ways to bless Paul in spite of Satan's best efforts to defeat him.

We have no idea what Paul's thorn was. Bible scholars have surmised answers for centuries, but none really knows. Pinpointing Paul's thorn serves no purpose. We know the wide variety of thorns because we all have one or more of our own. The point is, they remind us, as they reminded Paul, that we are weak earthen vessels. Our weakness humbles us and keeps us dependent upon God. Not a bad thing.

The word Paul uses for "torment me" in verse 7 actually means to crucify. As we identify with Christ dying on the Cross for our sins, we crucify the passions and desires of our fleshly or selfish nature while we live in a mind-set that follows the Spirit of Christ. The thorns of life sometimes torment us as we live for Him on this earth. When they do, we make sure everything but God's will for us remains dead.

Paul teaches in 2 Cor. 12:9-10 one of the key mysteries of service and ministry. That is, God's power sometimes works best in our lives at the point of our greatest weakness. We may prefer not to have the weakness, but somehow God's light may shine brightest through it. If so, our openness to His will and plan for our lives allows us to embrace even our weakness.

Why did Paul endure the weakness, insults, hardships, persecution, and difficulties? For Christ's sake! That's motivation for you to endure as well. "For when I am weak, then I am strong" (v. 10). Paul says much the same thing in 4:7, "But we have this treasure in jars of clay to show that this all-surpassing power is from God and not from us."

So does today end your quest for discovering life in the Spirit of Christ? No, quite the contrary. It's only beginning! Your quest has pointed you in the direction God wants to move you so that you might live the life you long for. As you have seen, striving and struggling do not produce this life for you. Rather, you receive it as a gift from God. You look to His guidance, accept His love, experience His purity, receive His power, and allow Him to develop a Christlike character in you.

I've waited 40 days to say this. Are you ready? *The life you long for is not about you!* It's about Christ and His example. The aim and focus is on others and the ways you can serve them in His name. It's not about finding yourself; it's about losing yourself. It's not about becoming strong; it's about coming to terms with your own weakness and finding your strength in Him. It's not about what you become; it's about what He becomes through you.

Life in the Spirit of Christ is a reflected life. You are like the moon. The moon is not a source of light. It only reflects the sun's light. In like manner, as you spend quality time with the Spirit of Christ, you reflect His life through yours. Over time, Christ is formed in you (Col. 1:27).

# DAY 40

**Remember:**
Life in the Spirit of Christ is a life of service.

*Therefore I will boast all the more gladly about my weaknesses, so that Christ's power may rest on me* (2 Cor. 12:9).

# CONCLUSION

Luke ended the Book of Acts in an interesting way. He spent the entire book telling of the acts of the Spirit of Christ as He worked in the Early Church. Then, without warning, the story ended. "Boldly, and without hindrance he preached the kingdom of God and taught about the Lord Jesus Christ" (Acts 28:31). It was as though Luke's account could not capture the ongoing nature of the work of the Spirit of Christ in God's Church.

People often refer to the continuation of the work of the Spirit in His Church following Luke's account as "Acts 29." That continuation reaches down to our age and our involvement with life in the Spirit of Christ. The Spirit continues to work with us just as He worked with the first disciples of Jesus.

The first disciples discovered life in the Spirit of Christ at Pentecost; we discover that life as well. They made each of the five discoveries we have made on our quest. They looked to the Spirit's guidance, accepted His love, experienced His purity, received His power, and allowed Him to develop a Christlike character in them. As a result of God's work in them, those first disciples changed their world. Their actions didn't bring about the change. God working through them made the difference. The same holds true for you. You'll change your world not through dedicated effort but because the Spirit of Christ works through you.

This is not the kind of book you read once then pass on to a friend or stick on a shelf. This is a book you read again and again as the Spirit of Christ reminds you of the truths of these five discoveries. It takes a lifetime to fully understand and apply them. As you grow and mature in His guidance, love, purity, power, and character, you realize the power to be free. You'll have both an "aha moment" of discovery and an ongoing

191

process of discovery for years to come.

Press forward on your quest as you continue to discover daily life in the Spirit of Christ! May your journey be fulfilling as you live in close personal relationship with Him. Blessings on you!